# Peace &
# WAR

*A collection of poems*

## Chosen by Michael Harrison &
## Christopher Stuart-Clark

Now the hard hand of the War-god was dealing out impartially
Death and agony: either side had its up and downs,
Its killings and fallen, alike; but neither dreamed of retreating.
In the halls of Jove the gods felt pity for all that pointless
Fury, to think that men should inflict such pains on their fellows.

Virgil, *Aeneid X*, translated by C. Day Lewis

Oxford University Press
Oxford New York Toronto

Oxford University Press, Great Clarendon Street, Oxford OX2 6DP

*Oxford   New York*
*Athens   Auckland   Bangkok   Bogota   Bombay*
*Buenos Aires   Calcutta   Cape Town   Dar es Salaam   Delhi*
*Florence   Hong Kong   Istanbul   Karachi*
*Kuala Lumpur   Madras   Madrid   Melbourne*
*Mexico City   Nairobi   Paris   Singapore*
*Taipei   Tokyo   Toronto   Warsaw*

and associated companies in
*Berlin   Ibadan*

*Oxford* is a trade mark of Oxford University Press

This selection and arrangement
© Michael Harrison and Christopher Stuart-Clark 1989

British Library Cataloguing in Publication Data
Peace and war
1. War poetry, English  2. English poetry
—20th century
1. Harrison, Michael
11. Stuart-Clark, Christopher
821'.914'080358     PR1195.W3
ISBN 0-19-276071-8 paperback

First published in 1989 in hardback and paperback
Hardback reprinted 1990, 1992
Paperback reprinted 1991, 1992
Paperback reprinted with new cover 1998

Typeset by Pentacor Ltd., High Wycombe, Bucks
Cover design by Bottle and Co. Design Consultants
Photograph supplied by Hulton Deutsch Collection Ltd
Printed in Hong Kong

Illustrated by Alan Marks

# Contents

5

## On this Island

Look, stranger, on this island now
The leaping light for your delight discovers,
Stand stable here
And silent be,
And through the channels of the ear
May wander like a river
The swaying sound of the sea.

Here at a small field's ending pause
When the chalk wall falls to the foam and its tall ledges
Oppose the pluck
And knock of the tide,

And the shingle scrambles after the sucking surf,
And a gull lodges
A moment on its sheer side.

Far off like floating seeds the ships
Diverge on urgent voluntary errands,
And this full view
Indeed may enter
And move in memory as now these clouds do,
That pass the harbour mirror
And all the summer through the water saunter.

*W. H. Auden*

# God's Grandeur

The world is charged with the grandeur of God.
    It will flame out, like shining from shook foil;
    It gathers to a greatness, like the ooze of oil
Crushed. Why do men then now not reck his rod?
Generations have trod, have trod, have trod;
    And all is seared with trade; bleared, smeared with toil;
    And wears man's smudge and shares man's smell: the
      soil
Is bare now, nor can foot feel, being shod.

And for all this, nature is never spent;
    There lives the dearest freshness deep down things;
And though the last lights off the black West went
    Oh, morning, at the brown brink eastward, springs—
Because the Holy Ghost over the bent
    World broods with warm breast and with ah! bright wings.

*Gerard Manley Hopkins*

# The Great Lover

I have been so great a lover: filled my days
So proudly with the splendour of Love's praise,
The pain, the calm, and the astonishment,
Desire illimitable, and still content,
And all dear names men use, to cheat despair,
For the perplexed and viewless streams that bear
Our hearts at random down the dark of life.
Now, ere the unthinking silence on that strife
Steals down, I would cheat drowsy Death so far,
My night shall be remembered for a star
That outshone all the suns of all men's days.
Shall I not crown them with immortal praise
Whom I have loved, who have given me, dared with me
High secrets, and in darkness knelt to see

The inenarrable godhead of delight?
Love is a flame:—we have beaconed the world's night.
A city:—and we have built it, these and I.
An emperor:—we have taught the world to die.
So, for their sakes I loved, ere I go hence,
And the high cause of Love's magnificence,
And to keep loyalties young, I'll write those names
Golden for ever, eagles, crying flames,
And set them as a banner, that men may know,
To dare the generations, burn, and blow
Out on the wind of Time, shining and streaming. . . .

These I have loved:
       White plates and cups, clean-gleaming,
Ringed with blue lines; and feathery, faery dust;
Wet roofs, beneath the lamp-light; the strong crust
Of friendly bread; and many-tasting food;
Rainbows; and the blue bitter smoke of wood;
And radiant raindrops couching in cool flowers;
And flowers themselves, that sway through sunny hours,
Dreaming of moths that drink them under the moon;
Then, the cool kindliness of sheets, that soon
Smooth away trouble; and the rough male kiss
Of blankets; grainy wood; live hair that is
Shining and free; blue-massing clouds; the keen
Unpassioned beauty of a great machine;
The benison of hot water; furs to touch;
The good smell of old clothes; and others such—
The comfortable smell of friendly fingers,
Hair's fragrance, and the musty reek that lingers
About dead leaves and last year's ferns. . . .
                       Dear names,
And thousand other throng to me! Royal flames;
Sweet water's dimpling laugh from tap or spring;
Holes in the ground; and voices that do sing;
Voices in laughter, too; and body's pain,
Soon turned to peace; and the deep-panting train;
Firm sands; the little dulling edge of foam

That browns and dwindles as the wave goes home;
And washen stones, gay for an hour; the cold
Graveness of iron; moist black earthen mould;
Sleep; and high places; footprints in the dew;
And oaks; and brown horse-chestnuts, glossy-new;
And new-peeled sticks; and shining pools on grass;—
All these have been my loves. And these shall pass,
Whatever passes not, in the great hour,
Nor all my passion, all my prayers, have power
To hold them with me through the gate of Death.
They'll play deserter, turn with the traitor breath,
Break the high bond we made, and sell Love's trust
And sacramented covenant to the dust.
——Oh, never a doubt but, somewhere, I shall wake,
And give what's left of love again, and make
New friends, now strangers. . . .
                              But the best I've known
Stays here, and changes, breaks, grows old, is blown
About the winds of the world, and fades from brains
Of living men, and dies.
                    Nothing remains.

O dear my loves, O faithless, once again
This one last gift I give: that after men
Shall know, and later lovers, far-removed,
Praise you, 'All these were lovely'; say, 'He loved.'

*Mataiea, 1914*
*Rupert Brooke*

# Words

I know you:
You are light as dreams,
Tough as oak,
Precious as gold,
As poppies and corn,
Or an old cloak:
Sweet as our birds
To the ear,
As the burnet rose
In the heat
Of Midsummer:
Strange as the races
Of dead and unborn:
Strange and sweet
Equally,
And familiar,
To the eye,
As the dearest faces
That a man knows,
And as lost homes are:
But though older far
Than oldest yew—
As our hills are, old—
Worn new
Again and again:
Young as our streams
After rain:
And as dear
As the earth which you prove
That we love.

*Edward Thomas*

# Day of These Days

Such a morning it is when love
leans through geranium windows
and calls with a cockerel's tongue.

When red-haired girls scamper like roses
over the rain-green grass;
and the sun drips honey.

When hedgerows grow venerable,
berries dry black as blood,
and holes suck in their bees.

Such a morning it is when mice
run whispering from the church,
dragging dropped ears of harvest.

When the partridge draws back his spring
and shoots like a buzzing arrow
over grained and mahogany fields.

When no table is bare,
and no beast dry,
and the tramp feeds on ribs of rabbit.

Such a day it is when time
piles up the hills like pumpkins,
and the streams run golden.

When all men smell good,
and the cheeks of girls
are as baked bread to the mouth.

As bread and beanflowers
the touch of their lips,
and their white teeth sweeter than cucumbers.

*Laurie Lee*

i thank You God for most this amazing
day for the leaping greenly spirits of trees
and a blue true dream of sky; and for everything
which is natural which is infinite which is yes

(i who have died am alive again today,
and this is the sun's birthday; this is the birth
day of life and of love and wings: and of the gay
great happening illimitably earth)

how should tasting touching hearing seeing
breathing any—lifted from the no
of all nothing—human merely being
doubt unimaginable You?

(now the ears of my ears awake and
now the eyes of my eyes are opened)

*e.e. cummings*


Where wast thou when I laid the foundations of the earth?
Declare, if thou hast understanding.
Who hast laid the measures thereof, if thou knowest?
Or who hast stretched the line upon it?
Whereupon are the foundations thereof fastened?
Or who laid the corner stone thereof?
When the morning stars sang together,
And all the sons of God shouted for joy?

*Job 38:4–7*
*The Bible: King James version*

# The Looker-on

. . . And ladders leaning against damson trees,
And idle spades beside old garden walls,
And broken sickles covered up in leaves,
And baskets wet with dew, waist deep in grass,
And spider webs across half-open gates . . .
    And memory of a moon, a giant rolling,
And, brown in moon's noonday, prolific oaks,
Glint of moonsilver on their solid acorns . . .
    And a fierce sun melting the fringed horizon,
Cold grass, hard apples fallen and forgotten,
And dew-logged thistledown . . . And crackling
        beechmast,
And plump matt mushrooms—beggars' harvest—white
As chalk, bland as a nut, and pink to break . . .
    And bonfire incense, and bracken gold as beech,
And bearded hedges, latest blackberries,
Half-ploughed stubble and dusty threshing yards,
And early nights, cloud multitudes on fire . . .
Dry noons, drenched dawns, deep scents, bright stars, lost
        thoughts . . .
    And empty orchards and wide open fields,
And robin solos in deserted woods,
And chimney smoke, and starry candlelight,
And far-off fields, and distance like the past,
And mossy silence, and the scent of leisure,
And spider webs across half-open gates,
And broken sickles buried under leaves,
And idle spades beside old garden walls,
And ladders leaning against damson trees, . . .

*Frank Kendon*

# The Glory

The glory of the beauty of the morning,—
The cuckoo crying over the untouched dew;
The blackbird that has found it, and the dove
That tempts me on to something sweeter than love;
White clouds ranged even and fair as new-mown hay;
The heat, the stir, the sublime vacancy
Of sky and meadow and forest and my own heart:—
The glory invites me, yet it leaves me scorning
All I can ever do, all I can be,
Beside the lovely of motion, shape, and hue,
The happiness I fancy fit to dwell
In beauty's presence. Shall I now this day
Begin to seek as far as heaven, as hell,
Wisdom or strength to match this beauty, start
And tread the pale dust pitted with small dark drops,
In hope to find whatever it is I seek,
Hearkening to short-lived happy-seeming things
That we know naught of, in the hazel copse?
Or must I be content with discontent
As larks and swallows are perhaps with wings?
And shall I ask at the day's end once more
What beauty is, and what I can have meant
By happiness? And shall I let all go,
Glad, weary, or both? Or shall I perhaps know
That I was happy oft and oft before,
Awhile forgetting how I am fast pent,
How dreary-swift, with naught to travel to,
Is Time? I cannot bite the day to the core.

*Edward Thomas*

# When I heard the learn'd astronomer

When I heard the learn'd astronomer,
When the proofs, the figures, were ranged in columns
    before me,
When I was shown the charts and diagrams, to add,
    divide, and measure them,
When I sitting heard the astronomer where he lectured
    with much applause in the lecture-room,
How soon unaccountable I became tired and sick,
Till rising and gliding out I wander'd off by myself,
In the mystical moist night-air, and from time to time,
Look'd up in perfect silence at the stars.

*Walt Whitman*


# Good

The old man comes out on the hill
and looks down to recall earlier days
in the valley. He sees the stream shine,
the church stand, hears the litter of
children's voices. A chill in the flesh
tells him that death is not far off
now: it is the shadow under the great boughs
of life. His garden has herbs growing.
The kestrel goes by with fresh prey
in its claws. The wind scatters the scent
of wild beans. The tractor operates
on the earth's body. His grandson is there
ploughing; his young wife fetches him
cakes and tea and a dark smile. It is well.

*R. S. Thomas*

# Rural Idyll

A mild man, God-fearing
tenor in the choir,
worships his acres;

sprays them with selective
death, and herds
cut calves in iron sheds
to fatten, as they smell
the enervating pasture;

breeds a million angel-
feathered souls in grids,
disinfected, their pallid
feet unsoiled by earth,
ramshackle roosting.

A prosperous farm. The silos
gleam in the sun; the church bells
carol a blessing over
oak beams, ancestral brick
gracious with leafage.

He husbands his clover
wife, who keeps the books;
their children
run and climb, secure
in eggs and milk and honey;

do as they're told, and sit
sedate and polished
in pews on Sunday.

*Margaret Toms*

# The Tuft of Flowers

I went to turn the grass once after one
Who mowed it in the dew before the sun.

The dew was gone that made his blade so keen
Before I came to view the levelled scene.

I looked for him behind an isle of trees;
I listened for his whetstone on the breeze.

But he had gone his way, the grass all mown,
And I must be, as he had been,—alone,

'As all must be,' I said within my heart,
'Whether they work together or apart.'

But as I said it, swift there passed me by
On noiseless wing a bewildered butterfly,

Seeking with memories grown dim o'er night
Some resting flower of yesterday's delight.

And once I marked his flight go round and round,
As where some flower lay withering on the ground.

And then he flew as far as eye could see,
And then on tremulous wing came back to me.

I thought of questions that have no reply,
And would have turned to toss the grass to dry;

But he turned first, and led my eye to look
At a tall tuft of flowers beside a brook,

A leaping tongue of bloom the scythe had spared
Beside a reedy brook the scythe had bared.

The mower in the dew had loved them thus,
By leaving them to flourish, not for us,

Nor yet to draw one thought of ours to him,
But from sheer morning gladness at the brim.

The butterfly and I had lit upon,
Nevertheless, a message from the dawn,

That made me hear the wakening birds around,
And hear his long scythe whispering to the ground,

And feel a spirit kindred to my own;
So that henceforth I worked no more alone;

But glad with him, I worked as with his aid,
And weary, sought at noon with him the shade;

And dreaming, as it were, held brotherly speech
With one whose thought I had not hoped to reach.

'Men work together,' I told him from the heart,
'Whether they work together or apart.'

*Robert Frost*


# I'll Have the Window Southward

I'll have the window southward.
A piece of land will I have
To dig and weed with a hoe.

I'll never be lured by clouds.
I'll enjoy free bird songs.
When the corns are ripe,
Come and share them on my table.

When someone asks why I live,
I just smile.

*Sang-yong Kim*
*translated from the Korean by Chang-soo Koh*

# Landscape

The ivy is green along the forest path;
The river gleams among the trees.

Wild birds perch on sun-lit boughs;
The white clouds saunter in the sky.

Crow-songs overflow the valley, and
The winds rush over the hills.

The streamlet is clear as jade
Beyond the winding forest paths.

The green mountains will live for a thousand years;
The river will flow for ten thousand
In this painted landscape. . . .

*Suk-jung Shin*
*translated from the Korean by Chang-soo Koh*


# Hills Surround Me

The hills surround me, and
Tell me to live my life,
Sowing the seeds,
Tilling the land.

Build a house below a hill,
Bear sons, bear daughters;
Plant pumpkins along the mud walls.
Live like wild roses,
Live like wormwood.

The hills surround me, and
Tell me to live like clouds,
Tell me to live like winds;
Life will soon wane like the moon!

*Mok-wol Park*
*translated from the Korean by Chang-soo Koh*

# Man

He breathes in the air, breathes in the early grass,
breathes the rushes while they stir,
every song while it can still be heard,
a warm woman's hand cupped beneath his head.
Breathes, breathes—but cannot breathe enough.

Breathes his mother—
                                        she who is the only one.
Breathes his country—
                                        he has no other.
Weeps, suffers, laughs, whistles,
and stands silent at the window, and sings till dusk,
and lovingly leafs through his brief life.

*Bulat Okudzhava*
*translated from the Russian by George Reavey*

# Fairy Tale

He built himself a house,
       his foundations,
       his stones,
       his walls,
       his roof overhead,
       his chimney and smoke,
       his view from the window.

He made himself a garden,
       his fence,
       his thyme,
       his earthworm,
       his evening dew.

He cut out his bit of sky above.

And he wrapped the garden in the sky
and the house in the garden
and packed the lot in a handkerchief
and went off
lone as an arctic fox
through the cold
unending
rain
into the world.

*Miroslav Holub*
*translated from the Czech by George Theiner*

# Legend

The blacksmith's boy went out with a rifle
and a black dog running behind.
Cobwebs snatched at his feet,
rivers hindered him,
thorn-branches caught at his eyes to make him blind
and the sky turned into an unlucky opal,
but he didn't mind,
I can break branches, I can swim rivers, I can stare out any
    spider I meet,
said he to his dog and his rifle.

The blacksmith's boy went over the paddocks
with his old black hat on his head.
Mountains jumped in his way,
rocks rolled down on him,
and the old crow cried, 'You'll soon be dead.'
And the rain came down like mattocks.
But he only said
I can climb mountains, I can dodge rocks, I can shoot an
    old crow any day,
and he went on over the paddocks.

When he came to the end of the day the sun began falling.
Up came the night ready to swallow him,
like the barrel of a gun,
like an old black hat,
like a black dog hungry to follow him.
Then the pigeon, the magpie and the dove began wailing
and the grass lay down to pillow him.
His rifle broke, his hat blew away and his dog was gone
and the sun was falling.

But in front of the night the rainbow stood on the
    mountain
just as his heart foretold.
He ran like a hare,
he climbed like a fox;

he caught it in his hands, the colours and the cold—
like a bar of ice, like the column of a fountain,
like a ring of gold.
The pigeon, the magpie and the dove flew up to stare
and the grass stood up again on the mountain.

The blacksmith's boy hung the rainbow on his shoulder
instead of his broken gun.
Lizards ran out to see,
snakes made way for him,
and the rainbow shone as brightly as the sun.
All the world said, Nobody is braver, nobody is bolder,
nobody else has done
anything to equal it. He went home as bold as he could be
with the swinging rainbow on his shoulder.

*Judith Wright*

## Nationality

I have grown past hate and bitterness,
I see the world as one;
Yet, though I can no longer hate,
My son is still my son.
    All men at God's round table sit,
    And all men must be fed;
    But this loaf in my hand,
    This loaf is my son's bread.

*Mary Gilmore*

# Song of the Rain

Night,
And the yellow pleasure of candle-light . . .
Old brown books and the kind fine face of the clock
Fogged in the veils of the fire—its cuddling tock.

The cat,
Greening her eyes on the flame-litten mat;
Wickedly wakeful she yawns at the rain
Bending the roses over the pane,
And a bird in my heart begins to sing
Over and over the same sweet thing—

*Safe in the house with my boyhood's love,*
*And our children asleep in the attic above.*

*Hugh McCrae*

# XII

Some say that love's a little boy,
    And some say it's a bird,
Some say it makes the world go round,
    And some say that's absurd,
And when I asked the man next-door,
    Who looked as if he knew,
His wife got very cross indeed,
    And said it wouldn't do.

Does it look like a pair of pyjamas,
    Or the ham in a temperance hotel?
Does its odour remind one of llamas,
    Or has it a comforting smell?
Is it prickly to touch as a hedge is,
    Or soft as eiderdown fluff?
Is it sharp or quite smooth at the edges?
    O tell me the truth about love.

Our history books refer to it
    In cryptic little notes,
It's quite a common topic on
    The Transatlantic boats;
I've found the subject mentioned in
    Accounts of suicides,
And even seen it scribbled on
    The backs of railway-guides.

Does it howl like a hungry Alsatian,
    Or boom like a military band?
Could one give a first-rate imitation
    On a saw or a Steinway Grand?
Is its singing at parties a riot?
    Does it only like Classical stuff?
Will it stop when one wants to be quiet?
    O tell me the truth about love.

I looked inside the summer-house;
     It wasn't ever there:
I tried the Thames at Maidenhead,
     And Brighton's bracing air.
I don't know what the blackbird sang,
     Or what the tulip said;
But it wasn't in the chicken-run,
     Or underneath the bed.

Can it pull extraordinary faces?
     Is it usually sick on a swing?
Does it spend all its time at the races,
     Or fiddling with pieces of string?
Has it views of its own about money?
     Does it think Patriotism enough?
Are its stories vulgar but funny?
     O tell me the truth about love.

When it comes, will it come without warning
     Just as I'm picking my nose?
Will it knock on my door in the morning,
     Or tread in the bus on my toes?
Will it come like a change in the weather?
     Will its greeting be courteous or rough?
Will it alter my life altogether?
     O tell me the truth about love.

*W. H. Auden*

## All day it has rained . . .

All day it has rained, and we on the edge of the moors
Have sprawled in our bell-tents, moody and dull as boors,
Groundsheets and blankets spread on the muddy ground
And from the first grey wakening we have found
No refuge from the skirmishing fine rain
And the wind that made the canvas heave and flap
And the taut wet guy-ropes ravel out and snap.

All day the rain has glided, wave and mist and dream,
Drenching the gorse and heather, a gossamer stream
Too light to stir the acorns that suddenly
Snatched from their cups by the wild south-westerly
Pattered against the tent and our upturned dreaming faces.
And we stretched out, unbuttoning our braces,
Smoking a Woodbine, darning dirty socks,
Reading the Sunday papers—I saw a fox
And mentioned it in the note I scribbled home;—
And we talked of girls, and dropping bombs on Rome,
And thought of the quiet dead and the loud celebrities

Exhorting us to slaughter, and the herded refugees;
—Yet thought softly, morosely of them, and as
    indifferently
As of ourselves or those whom we
For years have loved, and will again
Tomorrow maybe love; but now it is the rain
Possesses us entirely, the twilight and the rain.

And I can remember nothing dearer or more to my heart
Than the children I watched in the woods on Saturday
Shaking down burning chestnuts for the schoolyard's merry play,
Or the shaggy patient dog who followed me
By Sheet and Steep and up the wooded scree
To the Shoulder o' Mutton where Edward Thomas
    brooded long
On death and beauty—till a bullet stopped his song.

*Alun Lewis*

# Watching Post

A hill flank overlooking the Axe valley.
Among the stubble a farmer and I keep watch
For whatever may come to injure our countryside—
Light-signals, parachutes, bombs, or sea-invaders.
The moon looks over the hill's shoulder, and hope
Mans the old ramparts of an English night.

In a house down there was Marlborough born. One night
Monmouth marched to his ruin out of that valley.
Beneath our castled hill, where Britons kept watch,
Is a church where the Drakes, old lords of this country-
        side,
Sleep under their painted effigies. No invaders
Can dispute their legacy of toughness and hope.

Two counties away, over Bristol, the searchlights hope
To find what danger is in the air tonight.
Presently gunfire from Portland reaches our valley
Tapping like an ill-hung door in a draught. My watch
Says nearly twelve. All over the countryside
Moon-dazzled men are peering out for invaders.

The farmer and I talk for a while of invaders:
But soon we turn to crops—the annual hope,
Making of cider, prizes for ewes. Tonight
How many hearts along this war-mazed valley
Dream of a day when at peace they may work and watch
The small sufficient wonders of the countryside.

Image or fact, we both in the countryside
Have found our natural law, and until invaders
Come will answer its need: for both of us, hope
Means a harvest from small beginnings, who this night
While the moon sorts out into shadow and shape our
        valley,
A farmer and a poet, are keeping watch.

*C. Day Lewis*

# Lessons of the War: Naming of Parts

Today we have naming of parts. Yesterday,
We had daily cleaning. And tomorrow morning,
We shall have what to do after firing. But today,
Today we have naming of parts. Japonica
Glistens like coral in all of the neighbouring gardens,
  And today we have naming of parts.

This the lower sling swivel. And this
Is the upper sling swivel, whose use you will see,
When you are given your slings. And this is the piling swivel,
Which in your case you have not got. The branches
Hold in the gardens their silent, eloquent gestures,
  Which in our case we have not got.

This is the safety-catch, which is always released
With an easy flick of the thumb. And please do not let me
See anyone using his finger. You can do it quite easy
If you have any strength in your thumb. The blossoms
Are fragile and motionless, never letting anyone see
  Any of them using their finger.

And this you can see is the bolt. The purpose of this
Is to open the breech, as you see. We can slide it
Rapidly backwards and forwards: we call this
Easing the spring. And rapidly backwards and forwards
The early bees are assaulting and fumbling the flowers:
  They call it easing the Spring.

They call it easing the Spring: it is perfectly easy
If you have any strength in your thumb: like the bolt,
And the breech, and the cocking-piece, and the point of balance,
Which in our case we have not got; and the almond-blossom
Silent in all of the gardens and the bees going backwards
    and forwards
  For today we have naming of parts.

*Henry Reed*

# Report to the Valley Camp

We went to reconnoitre
up Fox Hill, looking out
for any file or scout,
high pass, wooded stream-crossing,
fortified place, or any important feature.

So, sir, we climbed the crags.
What we saw then amazed us. Clouds go by
like close companions. Swifts and merlins fly
bathed in those regions as their own.
But most of all, the distance! and the height!

What of strategic value?
But the moist clouds—as close as me to you!
It's bare up there, moorland. A rendez-vous
with the birds' landscape, with the sun and moon.
You're a king there, believe in power like flight.

Yes, sir, strategic: no, we didn't see
marks of activity or groups of men
or anything suspicious. Now and then
we heard the lark, in acres of air. I think
this land is more important than we knew.
I saw no strongholds—but the view! The view!

*Jenny King*


# The Last Day of Leave
## (1916)

We five looked out over the moor
At rough hills blurred with haze, and a still sea:
Our tragic day, bountiful from the first.

We would spend it by the lily lake
(High in a fold beyond the farthest ridge),
Following the cart-track till it faded out.

The time of berries and bell-heather;
Yet all that morning nobody went by
But shepherds and one old man carting turfs.

We were in love: he with her, she with him,
And I, the youngest one, the odd man out,
As deep in love with a yet nameless muse.

No cloud; larks and heath-butterflies,
And herons undisturbed fishing the streams;
A slow cool breeze that hardly stirred the grass.

When we hurried down the rocky slope,
A flock of ewes galloping off in terror,
There shone the waterlilies, yellow and white.

Deep water and a shelving bank.
Off went our clothes and in we went, all five,
Diving like trout between the lily groves.

The basket had been nobly filled:
Wine and fresh rolls, chicken and pineapple—
Our braggadocio under the threat of war.

The fire on which we boiled our kettle
We fed with ling and rotten blackthorn root;
And the coffee tasted memorably of peat.

Two of us might stray off together
But never less than three kept by the fire,
Focus of our uncertain destinies.

We spoke little, our minds in tune—
A sigh or laugh would settle any theme;
The sun so hot it made the rocks quiver.

But when it rolled down level with us,
Four pairs of eyes sought mine as if appealing
For a blind-fate-aversive afterword:—

'Do you remember the lily lake?'
We were all there, all five of us in love,
Not one yet killed, widowed or broken-hearted.

*Robert Graves*

## Autumn, 1939

The beech boles whiten in the swollen stream;
Their red leaves, shaken from the creaking boughs,
Float down the flooded meadow, half in dream,
Seen in a mirror cracked by broken vows,

Water-logged, slower, deeper, swirling down
Between the indifferent hills who also saw
Old jaundiced knights jog listlessly to town
To fight for love in some unreal war.

Black leaves are piled against the roaring weir;
Dark closes round the manor and the hut;
The dead knight moulders on his rotting bier,
And one by one the warped old casements shut.

*Alun Lewis*

## Waiting for the Barbarians

What are we waiting for, gathered in the market-place?

   The barbarians are to arrive today.

Why so little activity in the senate?
Why do the senators sit there without legislating?

   Because the barbarians will arrive today.
   What laws should the senators make now?
   The barbarians, when they come, will do the legislating.

Why has our emperor risen so early,
and why does he sit at the largest gate of the city
on the throne, in state, wearing the crown?

Because the barbarians will arrive today.
And the emperor is waiting to receive
their leader. He has even prepared
a parchment for him. There
he has given him many titles and names.

Why did our two consuls and our praetors go out
today in the scarlet, the embroidered, togas?
Why did they wear bracelets with so many amethysts,
and rings with brilliant sparkling emeralds?
Why today do they carry precious staves
splendidly inlaid with silver and gold?

    Because the barbarians will arrive today;
    and such things dazzle barbarians.

And why don't the worthy orators come as always
to make their speeches, say what they have to say?

    Because the barbarians will arrive today;
    and they are bored by eloquence and public speaking.

What does this sudden uneasiness mean,
and this confusion? (How grave the faces have become!)
Why are the streets and squares rapidly emptying,
and why is everyone going back home so lost in thought?

    Because it is night and the barbarians have not come.
    And some men have arrived from the frontiers
    and they say that barbarians don't exist any longer.

And now, what will become of us without barbarians?
They were a kind of solution.

*C. P. Cavafy*
*Translated from the Greek by Edmund Keeley and Philip*
    *Sherrard*

# Peace

Now, God be thanked Who has matched us with His hour,
   And caught our youth, and wakened us from sleeping,
With hand made sure, clear eye, and sharpened power,
   To turn, as swimmers into cleanness leaping,
Glad from a world grown old and cold and weary,
   Leave the sick hearts that honour could not move,
And half-men, and their dirty songs and dreary,
   And all the little emptiness of love!

Oh! we, who have known shame, we have found release there,
   Where there's no ill, no grief, but sleep has mending.
      Naught broken save this body, lost but breath;
Nothing to shake the laughing heart's long peace there
   But only agony, and that has ending;
      And the worst friend and enemy is but Death.

*Rupert Brooke*

# The Soldier

If I should die, think only this of me:
　　That there's some corner of a foreign field
That is for ever England. There shall be
　　In that rich earth a richer dust concealed;
A dust whom England bore, shaped, made aware,
　　Gave, once, her flowers to love, her ways to roam,
A body of England's, breathing English air,
　　Washed by the rivers, blest by suns of home.

And think, this heart, all evil shed away,
　　A pulse in the eternal mind, no less
　　　　Gives somewhere back the thoughts by England given;
Her sights and sounds; dreams happy as her day;
　　And laughter, learnt of friends; and gentleness,
　　　　In hearts at peace, under an English heaven.

*Rupert Brooke*

# Stanzas

When a man hath no freedom to fight for at home,
    Let him combat for that of his neighbours;
Let him think of the glories of Greece and of Rome,
    And get knocked on the head for his labours.

To do good to mankind is the chivalrous plan,
    And is always as nobly requited;
Then battle for freedom wherever you can,
    And, if not shot or hanged, you'll get knighted.

*Lord Byron*


'next to of course god america i
love you land of the pilgrims' and so forth oh
say can you see by the dawn's early my
country 'tis of centuries come and go
and are no more what of it we should worry
in every language even deafanddumb
thy sons acclaim your glorious name by gorry
by jingo by gee by gosh by gum
why talk of beauty what could be more beaut-
iful than these heroic happy dead
who rushed like lions to the roaring slaughter
they did not stop to think they died instead
then shall the voice of liberty be mute?'

He spoke. And drank rapidly a glass of water

*e. e. cummings*

# To Lucasta, Going to the Wars

Tell me not, sweet, I am unkind,
    That from the nunnery
Of thy chaste breast and quiet mind
    To war and arms I fly.

True, a new mistress now I chase,
    The first foe in the field;
And with a stronger faith embrace
    A sword, a horse, a shield.

Yet this inconstancy is such
    As you too shall adore;
I could not love thee, dear, so much,
    Loved I not honour more.

*Richard Lovelace*

Demetrius fled the fight in fear.
And lost his weapons. Once at home,
His mother stabbed him with a spear
Through his side, and said to him:

'Die. Let Sparta feel no shame.
My milk fed cowards in her name.'

*Erycius of Cyzicus*

Demaeneta sent eight sons
To fight the ranks of the foe.
She buried them all at once,
Her mourning saw no tears flow.

One sentence she said only:
'Sparta, I bore them for thee.'

*Dioscorides*

# Route March

All the hills and vales along
Earth is bursting into song,
And the singers are the chaps
Who are going to die perhaps.
 O sing, marching men,
 Till the valleys ring again.
 Give your gladness to earth's keeping,
 So be glad, when you are sleeping.

Cast away regret and rue,
Think what you are marching to.
Little live, great pass.
Jesus Christ and Barabbas
Were found the same day.
This died, that went his way.
 So sing with joyful breath.
 For why, you are going to death.
 Teeming earth will surely store
 All the gladness that you pour.

Earth that never doubts nor fears,
Earth that knows of death, not tears,
Earth that bore with joyful ease
Hemlock for Socrates,
Earth that blossomed and was glad
'Neath the cross that Christ had,
Shall rejoice and blossom too
When the bullet reaches you.
 Wherefore, men marching
 On the road to death, sing!
 Pour your gladness on earth's head,
 So be merry, so be dead.

From the hills and valleys earth
Shouts back the sound of mirth,
Tramp of feet and lilt of song
Ringing all the road along.

All the music of their going,
Ringing swinging glad song-throwing,
Earth will echo still, when foot
Lies numb and voice mute.
On, marching men, on
To the gates of death with song.
Sow your gladness for earth's reaping,
So you may be glad, though sleeping.
Strew your gladness on earth's bed,
So be merry, so be dead.

*Charles Sorley*


I will sing unto the Lord, for he hath triumphed gloriously:
the horse and his rider hath he thrown into the sea.
The Lord is my strength and song, and he is become my
salvation:
he is my God and I will prepare him an habitation;
my father's God, and I will exalt him.
The Lord is a man of war:
the Lord is his name.
Pharaoh's chariots and his host hath he cast into the sea:
his chosen captains also are drowned in the Red Sea.
The depths have covered them:
they sank into the bottom as a stone.
Thy right hand, O Lord, is become glorious in power:
thy right hand. O Lord, hath dashed in pieces the
enemy.
And in the greatness of thine excellency thou hast
overthrown them that rose up against thee:
thou sentest forth thy wrath, which consumed them as
stubble.

And with the blast of thy nostrils the waters were gathered
     together,
the floods stood upright as an heap,
and the depths were congealed in the heart of the sea.
The enemy said, I will pursue, I will overtake, I will divide
     the spoil;
my lust shall be satisfied upon them; I will draw my sword,
my hand shall destroy them.
Thou didst blow with thy wind, the sea covered them:
     they sank as lead in the mighty waters.
Who is like unto thee, O Lord, among the gods?
Who is like thee, glorious in holiness,
fearful in praises,
doing wonders?

*Exodus 15 : I–II*
*The Bible: King James Version*


# On the Late Massacre in Piedmont

Avenge, O Lord, thy slaughtered saints, whose bones
   Lie scattered on the Alpine mountains cold,
   Even them who kept thy truth so pure of old
   When all our fathers worshipped stocks and stones,
Forget not; in thy book record their groans
   Who were thy sheep and in their ancient fold
   Slain by the bloody Piedmontese that rolled
   Mother with infant down the rocks. Their moans
   The vales redoubled to the hills, and they
   To Heaven. Their martyred blood and ashes sow
   O'er all th' Italian fields where still doth sway
The triple tyrant, that from these may grow
   A hundredfold, who having learnt thy way,
   Early may fly the Babylonian woe.

*John Milton*

# Ye Mariners of England

Ye Mariners of England
 That guard our native seas!
Whose flag has braved a thousand years
 The battle and the breeze!
Your glorious standard launch again
 To match another foe;
And sweep through the deep,
 While the stormy winds do blow!
While the battle rages loud and long
 And the stormy winds do blow.

The spirits of your fathers
 Shall start from every wave—
For the deck it was their field of fame,
 And Ocean was their grave:
Where Blake and mighty Nelson fell
 Your manly hearts shall glow,
As ye sweep through the deep,
 While the stormy winds do blow!
While the battle rages loud and long
 And the stormy winds do blow.

Britannia needs no bulwarks,
 No towers along the steep;
Her march is o'er the mountain-waves,
 Her home is on the deep.
With thunders from her native oak
 She quells the floods below,
As they roar on the shore,
 When the stormy winds do blow!
When the battle rages loud and long,
 And the stormy winds do blow.

The meteor flag of England
 Shall yet terrific burn;
Till danger's troubled night depart
 And the star of peace return.

Then, then, ye ocean-warriors!
   Our song and feast shall flow
To the fame of your name,
   When the storm has ceased to blow!
When the fiery fight is heard no more,
   And the storm has ceased to blow.

*Thomas Campbell*


# Henry V at the Siege of Harfleur

Once more unto the breach, dear friends, once more;
Or close the wall up with our English dead!
In peace there's nothing so becomes a man
As modest stillness and humility:
But when the blast of war blows in our ears,
Then imitate the action of the tiger;
Stiffen the sinews, summon up the blood,
Disguise fair nature with hard-favour'd rage;
Then lend the eye a terrible aspect;
Let it pry through the portage of the head
Like the brass cannon; let the brow o'erwhelm it
As fearfully as doth a galled rock
O'erhang and jutty his confounded base,
Swill'd with the wild and wasteful ocean.
Now set the teeth and stretch the nostril wide,
Hold hard the breath, and bend up every spirit
To his full height! On, on you noblest English!
Whose blood is fet from fathers of war-proof;
Fathers that, like so many Alexanders,
Have in these parts from morn till even fought,
And sheath'd their swords for lack of argument.
Dishonour not your mothers; now attest
That those whom you call'd fathers did beget you.
Be copy now to men of grosser blood,
And teach them how to war. And you, good yeomen,

Whose limbs were made in England, show us here
The mettle of your pasture; let us swear
That you are worth your breeding; which I doubt not;
For there is none of you so mean and base
That hath not noble lustre in your eyes.
I see you stand like greyhounds in the slips,
Straining upon the start. The game's afoot:
Follow your spirit; and upon this charge
Cry 'God for Harry! England and Saint George!'

*William Shakespeare*


## Epitaph on a Jacobite
(1845)

To my true king I offered free from stain
Courage and faith; vain faith, and courage vain.
For him, I threw lands, honours, wealth, away.
And one dear hope, that was more prized than they.
For him I languished in a foreign clime,
Grey-haired with sorrow in my manhood's prime;
Heard on Lavernia Scargill's whispering trees,
And pined by Arno for my lovelier Tees;
Beheld each night my home in fevered sleep,
Each morning started from the dream to weep;
Till God who saw me tried too sorely gave
The resting place I asked, an early grave,
Oh thou, whom chance leads to this nameless stone,
From that proud country which was once mine own,
By those white cliffs I never more must see,
By that dear language which I spake like thee,
Forget all feuds, and shed one English tear
O'er English dust. A broken heart lies here.

*Lord Macaulay*

# Before Agincourt

*Westmoreland.*          O! that we now had here
     But one ten thousand of those men in England
     That do no work to-day.
*King Henry.*          What's he that wishes so?
     My cousin Westmoreland? No, my fair cousin:
     If we are mark'd to die, we are enow
     To do our country loss; and if to live,
     The fewer men, the greater share of honour.
     God's will! I pray thee, wish not one man more.
     By Jove, I am not covetous for gold,
     Nor care I who doth feed upon my cost;
     It yearns me not if men my garments wear;
     Such outward things dwell not in my desires:
     But if it be a sin to covet honour,
     I am the most offending soul alive.
     No, faith, my coz, wish not a man from England:
     God's peace! I would not lose so great an honour
     As one man more, methinks, would share from me,
     For the best hope I have. O! do not wish one more:
     Rather proclaim it, Westmoreland, through my host,
     That he which hath no stomach to this fight,
     Let him depart; his passport shall be made,
     And crowns for convoy put into his purse:
     We would not die in that man's company
     That fears his fellowship to die with us.
     This day is call'd the feast of Crispian:
     He that outlives this day, and comes safe home,
     Will stand a tip-toe when this day is nam'd,
     And rouse him at the name of Crispian.
     He that shall live this day, and see old age,
     Will yearly on the vigil feast his neighbours,
     And say, 'To-morrow is Saint Crispian:'
     Then will he strip his sleeve and show his scars,
     And say, 'These wounds I had on Crispin's day.'
     Old men forget: yet all shall be forgot,

But he'll remember with advantages
What feats he did that day. Then shall our names,
Familiar in his mouth as household words,
Harry the king, Bedford and Exeter,
Warwick and Talbot, Salisbury and Gloucester,
Be in their flowing cups freshly remember'd.
This story shall the good man teach his son;
And Crispin Crispian shall ne'er go by,
From this day to the ending of the world,
But we in it shall be remembered;
We few, we happy few, we band of brothers;
For he to-day that sheds his blood with me
Shall be my brother; be he ne'er so vile
This day shall gentle his condition:
And gentlemen in England, now a-bed,
Shall think themselves accurs'd they were not here,
And hold their manhoods cheap whiles any speaks
That fought with us upon Saint Crispin's day.

*William Shakespeare*

# After Blenheim

It was a summer evening,
  Old Kaspar's work was done,
And he before his cottage door
  Was sitting in the sun;
And by him sported on the green
His little grandchild Wilhelmine.

She saw her brother Peterkin
  Roll something large and round
Which he beside the rivulet
  In playing there had found;
He came to ask what he had found
That was so large and smooth and round.

Old Kaspar took it from the boy
  Who stood expectant by;
And then the old man shook his head,
  And with a natural sigh
''Tis some poor fellow's skull,' said he;
'Who fell in the great victory.

'I find them in the garden,
  For there's many here about;
And often when I go to plough
  The ploughshare turns them out.
For many thousand men,' said he,
'Were slain in that great victory.'

'Now tell us what 'twas all about,'
  Young Peterkin he cries;
And little Wilhelmine looks up
  With wonder-waiting eyes;
'Now tell us all about the war,
And what they fought each other for.'

'It was the English,' Kaspar cried,
  'Who put the French to rout;
But what they fought each other for

I could not well make out.
　But everybody said,' quoth he,
'That 'twas a famous victory.

'My father lived at Blenheim then,
　　Yon little stream hard by;
They burnt his dwelling to the ground,
　　And he was forced to fly:
So with his wife and child he fled,
Nor had he where to rest his head.

'With fire and sword the country round
　　Was wasted far and wide,
And many a childing mother then
　　And new-born baby died:
But things like that, you know, must be
At every famous victory.

'They say it was a shocking sight
　　After the field was won;
For many thousand bodies here
　　Lay rotting in the sun:
But things like that, you know, must be
After a famous victory.

'Great praise the Duke of Marlbro' won
　　And our good Prince Eugene;'
'Why, 'twas a very wicked thing!'
　　Said little Wilhelmine;
'Nay . . . nay . . . my little girl,' quoth he,
'It was a famous victory.

'And everybody praised the Duke
　　Who this great fight did win.'
'But what good came of it at last?'
　　Quoth little Peterkin:—
'Why, that I cannot tell,' said he,
'But 'twas a famous victory!'

*Robert Southey*

# Before Action

By all the glories of the day
   And the cool evening's benison,
By that last sunset touch that lay
   Upon the hills when day was done,
By beauty lavishly outpoured
   And blessings carelessly received,
By all the days that I have lived
   Make me a soldier, Lord.

By all of man's hopes and fears,
   And all the wonders poets sing,
The laughter of unclouded years,
   And every sad and lovely thing;
By the romantic ages stored
   With high endeavour that was his,
By all his mad catastrophes
   Make me a man, O Lord.

I, that on my familiar hill
   Saw with uncomprehending eyes
A hundred of Thy sunsets spill
   Their fresh and sanguine sacrifice,
Ere the sun swings his noonday sword
   Must say goodbye to all of this—
By all delights that I shall miss,
   Help me to die, O Lord.

*W. N. Hodgson*


# Does it Matter?

Does it matter?—losing your legs? . . .
For people will always be kind,
And you need not show that you mind
When the others come in after hunting
To gobble their muffins and eggs.

Does it matter?—losing your sight? . . .
There's such splendid work for the blind;
And people will always be kind,
As you sit on the terrace remembering
And turning your face to the light.

Do they matter?—those dreams from the pit? . . .
You can drink and forget and be glad,
And people won't say that you're mad;
For they'll know that you've fought for your country,
And no one will worry a bit.

*Siegfried Sassoon*


# Spring 1942

Once as we were sitting by
The falling sun, the thickening air,
The chaplain came against the sky
And quietly took a vacant chair.

And under the tobacco smoke:
'Freedom,' he said, and 'Good' and 'Duty.'
We stared as though a savage spoke.
The scene took on a singular beauty.

And we made no reply to that
Obscure, remote communication,
But only looked out where the flat
Meadow dissolved in vegetation.

And thought: O sick, insatiable
And constant lust; O death, our future;
O revolution in the whole
Of human use of man and nature!

*Roy Fuller*

'This town, now, yes, Mother,
is happier than the Greeks—
They came here to the banks of the Scamander,
and tens of thousands died. For what?
No man had moved their land-marks
or laid siege to their high-walled towns.
But those whom war took never saw their children.
No wife with gentle hand shrouded them for their grave.
They lie in a strange land. And in their homes
are sorrows too, the very same.
Lonely women who died. Old men who waited
for sons that never came.
This is the glorious victory they won.
But we—we Trojans died to save our people.
Oh, fly from war if you are wise. But if war comes,
to die well is to win the victor's crown.'

*Euripides, The Trojan Women*
*translated from the Ancient Greek by Edith Hamilton*

# Dulce et Decorum est

Bent double, like old beggars under sacks,
Knock-kneed, coughing like hags, we cursed through sludge,
Till on the haunting flares we turned our backs,
And towards our distant rest began to trudge.
Men marched asleep. Many had lost their boots,
But limped on, blood-shod. All went lame, all blind;
Drunk with fatigue; deaf even to the hoots
Of gas-shells dropping softly behind.

Gas! Gas! Quick boys!—An ecstasy of fumbling,
Fitting the clumsy helmets just in time,
But someone still was yelling out and stumbling
And floundering like a man in fire or lime.—
Dim through the misty panes and thick green light,
As under a green sea, I saw him drowning.
In all my dreams, before my helpless sight,
He plunges at me, guttering, choking, drowning.

If in some smothering dreams, you too could pace
Behind the wagon that we flung him in,
And watch the white eyes writhing in his face,
His hanging face, like a devil's sick of sin;
If you could hear, at every jolt, the blood
Come gargling from the froth-corrupted lungs,
Obscene as cancer, bitter as the cud
Of vile, incurable sores on innocent tongues,—
My friend, you would not tell with such high zest
To children ardent for some desperate glory,
The old Lie: *Dulce et decorum est
Pro patria mori.*

*Wilfred Owen*

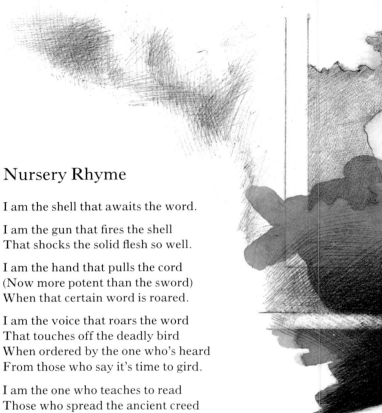

# Nursery Rhyme

I am the shell that awaits the word.

I am the gun that fires the shell
That shocks the solid flesh so well.

I am the hand that pulls the cord
(Now more potent than the sword)
When that certain word is roared.

I am the voice that roars the word
That touches off the deadly bird
When ordered by the one who's heard
From those who say it's time to gird.

I am the one who teaches to read
Those who spread the ancient creed
To aid the ones who feed the need
Of the hand that's forced to heed
The word that fathers forth the deed.

I am the one who works the drill,
Who tills the soil, who takes his pill,
Who backs with tax the shell he makes
To feed the hand of him who takes
The word that comes from certain men
Who give the word to fire when.

Who is this one who gives the word
To lift aloft the deadly bird?

I am the one behind the shell.

*Leo Hamalian*

Cruelty has a Human Heart,
And Jealousy a Human Face;
Terror the Human Form Divine,
And Secrecy the Human Dress.

The Human Dress is forged Iron,
The Human Form a fiery Forge,
The Human Face a Furnace seal'd,
The Human Heart its hungry Gorge.

*William Blake*

# The Hand that Signed the Paper

The hand that signed the paper felled a city;
Five sovereign fingers taxed the breath,
Doubled the globe of dead and halved a country;
These five kings did a king to death.

The mighty hand leads to a sloping shoulder,
The finger joints are cramped with chalk;
A goose's quill has put an end to murder
That put an end to talk.

The hand that signed the treaty bred a fever,
And famine grew, and locusts came;
Great is the hand that holds dominion over
Man by a scribbled name.

The five kings count the dead but do not soften
The crusted wound nor stroke the brow;
A hand rules pity as a hand rules heaven;
Hands have no tears to flow.

*Dylan Thomas*

# The Inflatable Globe

When the allegorical man came calling,
He told us all he would show us a trick,
And he showed us a flat but inflatable ball.
'Look at this ball,' he told us all;
'Look at the lines marked out on this ball.'
We looked at the ball and the lines on the ball:
England was red, and France was blue;
Germany orange and Russia brown:
'Look at this ball,' he told us all,
'With a blow of my breath I inflate this ball.'
He blew, and it bounced, and bouncing, falling,
He bounced it against the wall with a kick.
'But without my breath it will flatten and fall,'
Said the allegorical man; and down
Flat came his hand and squashed the ball,
And it fell on the floor with no life at all
Once his breath had gone out of the ball . . .
It seemed to us all a stupid trick.

*Theodore Spencer*

# Epitaph on a Tyrant

Perfection, of a kind, was what he was after,
And the poetry he invented was easy to understand;
He knew human folly like the back of his hand,
And was greatly interested in armies and fleets;
When he laughed, respectable senators burst with laughter,
And when he cried the little children died in the streets.

*W. H. Auden*

How few of us are left, how few!
Why do we not go back?
Were it not for our prince and his concerns,
What should we be doing here in the dew?

How few of us are left, how few!
Why do we not go back?
Were it not for our prince's own concerns,
What should we be doing here in the mud?

*from Book of Songs*
*translated from the Chinese by Arthur Waley*


# Crazed Man in Concentration Camp

All through the march, besides bag and blanket
he carried in his hands two packages of empty boxes,
and when the company halted for a couple of minutes
he laid the two packages of empty boxes neatly at each side,
being careful not to damage or break either of them,
the parcels were of
ornamental boxes
dovetailed by sizes each to each
and tied together with packing-cord,
the top box with a picture on it.
When the truck was about to start, the sergeant
shouted something in sergeant's language,
they sprang up suddenly,
and one of the boxes rolled down to the wheel,
the smallest one, the one with the picture:
'It's fallen,' he said and made to go after it,
but the truck moved off
and his companions held his hands
while his hands held the two packages of boxes
and his tears trailed down his jacket.
'It's fallen,' he said that evening in the queue—
and it meant nothing to him to be shot dead.

*Agnes Gergely*
*translated from the Hungarian by Edwin Morgan*

# The Next War
*To Sacheverell*
*(November 1918)*

The long war had ended.
Its miseries had grown faded.
Deaf men became difficult to talk to,
Heroes became bores.
Those alchemists
Who had converted blood into gold
Had grown elderly.
But they held a meeting,
Saying,
'We think perhaps we ought
To put up tombs
Or erect altars
To those brave lads
Who were so willingly burnt,
Or blinded,
Or maimed,
Who lost all likeness to a living thing,
Or were blown to bleeding patches of flesh
For our sakes.
It would look well.
Or we might even educate the children.'
But the richest of these wizards
Coughed gently;
And he said:
    'I have always been to the front
    —In private enterprise—,
    I yield in public spirit
    To no man.
    I think yours is a very good idea
    —A capital idea—
    And not too costly . . .

    But it seems to me
    That the cause for which we fought

Is again endangered.
What more fitting memorial for the fallen
Than that their children
Should fall for the same cause?'

Rushing eagerly into the street,
The kindly old gentlemen cried
To the young:
  'Will you sacrifice
  Through your lethargy
  What your fathers died to gain?
  The world *must* be made safe for the young!'

And the children
Went. . . .

*Osbert Sitwell*


# On the Tomb of the Spartan Dead at Thermopylae

Stranger, tell the Spartans how we die:
Obedient to their laws, here we lie.

# Ultima Ratio Regum

The guns spell money's ultimate reason
In letters of lead on the Spring hillside.
But the boy lying dead under the olive trees
Was too young and too silly
To have been notable to their important eye.
He was a better target for a kiss.

When he lived, tall factory hooters never summoned him
Nor did restaurant plate-glass doors revolve to wave him in.
His name never appeared in the papers.
The world maintained its traditional wall
Round the dead with their gold sunk deep as a well,
Whilst his life, intangible as a Stock Exchange rumour,
    drifted outside.

O too lightly he threw down his cap
One day when the breeze threw petals from the trees.
The unflowering wall sprouted with guns,
Machine-gun anger quickly scythed the grasses;
Flags and leaves fell from hands and branches;
The tweed cap rotted in the nettles.

Consider his life which was valueless
In terms of employment, hotel ledgers, new files.
Consider. One bullet in ten thousand kills a man.
Ask. Was so much expenditure justified
On the death of one so young, and so silly
Lying under the olive trees, O world, O death?

*Stephen Spender*

# Fighting South of the Ramparts

They fought south of the ramparts,
They died north of the wall.
They died in the moors and were not buried.
Their flesh was the food of crows.
'Tell the crows we are not afraid;
We have died in the moors and cannot be buried.
Crows, how can our bodies escape you?'
The waters flowed deep
And the rushes in the pool were dark.
The riders fought and were slain;
Their horses wander neighing.
By the bridge there was a house.
Was it south, was it north?
The harvest was never gathered.
How can we give you your offerings?
You served your Prince faithfully,
Though all in vain.
I think of you, faithful soldiers;
Your service shall not be forgotten.
For in the morning you went out to battle
And at night you did not return.

*From Book of Songs*
*translated from the Chinese by Arthur Waley*

# On the Death of Young Guerillas

You called me, but I made no response in that night;
I feared you, you whose power strikes with terror.
You killed my children with a blunt spear,
You held me back so that I may not bury them.
The soil disgorges them:
Wherever I go I find their bodies scattered.
Could it be that you are tired of the old ones
Who reappear in the valley of dreams?
Could it be they whet your appetite with their flesh?
Could it be you are blind in your destruction?

*Mazisi Kunene*

# A Paper Soldier

In our world there lived a soldier.
He was extremely handsome, very brave,
but he happened to be a children's toy—
for he was merely a paper soldier.

He wished to refashion all the world,
to make each individual happy,
but he dangled over a child's cot,
for he was merely a paper soldier.

He would have dashed through smoke and fire,
and given his life for you twice over,
but you only derided him and laughed—
for he was merely a paper soldier.

You were unwilling to entrust
him with your most important secrets.
And why did you not trust him? Oh, just
because he was a paper soldier.

And kicking against his wretched lot,
he thirsted for a life less tranquil,
and kept demanding: 'Fire! Yes, Fire!'
forgetting he was a paper soldier.

Into fire? All right. Why not plunge in?
And bravely forward he marched off.
And there he perished, nothing won—
for he was merely a paper soldier.

*Bulat Okudzhava*
*translated from the Russian by George Reavey*


# Winter Warfare

Colonel Cold strode up the Line
   (tabs of rime and spurs of ice);
stiffened all that met his glare:
   horses, men, and lice.

Visited a forward post,
   left them burning, ear to foot;
fingers stuck to biting steel,
   toes to frozen boot.

Stalked on into No Man's Land,
   turned the wire to fleecy wool,
iron stakes to sugar sticks
   snapping at a pull.

Those who watched with hoary eyes
   saw two figures gleaming there;
Hauptmann Kälte, Colonel Cold,
   gaunt in the grey air.

Stiffly, tinkling spurs they moved,
   glassy-eyed, with glinting heel
stabbing those who lingered there
   torn by screaming steel.

*Edgell Rickword*

# Buttons

I have been watching the war map slammed up for
    advertising in front of the newspaper office.
Buttons—red and yellow buttons—black and blue
    buttons— are shoved back and forth across the map.

A laughing young man, sunny with freckles,
Climbs a ladder, yells a joke to somebody in the crowd,
And then fixes a yellow button one inch west
And follows the yellow button with a black button one inch west.

(Ten thousand men and boys twist on their bodies in a red
    soak along a river edge,
Gasping of wounds, calling for water, some rattling death
    in their throats.)
Who by Christ would guess what it cost to move two
    buttons one inch west on the war map here in front of
    the newspaper office where the freckle-faced young
    man is laughing at us?

*Carl Sandburg*

# The Question

Perhaps I killed a man to-day,
   I cannot tell: I do not know,
But bare three hundred yards away,
   Where weeping willows grow,
Fell sudden silence on the heels
   Of my last shot, whose echoes rang
Along the Rhine. A silence steals
   Across the river, save the bang
Of distant, screaming shell;
   The tapping of the Spandau
Comes no more; brief quiet fell
   Where weeping willows grow.

Perhaps I killed a man to-day,
   The secret's hid, forever laid
Among those willows o'er the way;
   Here, beneath the quiet shade
Of a heeled, abandoned tank,
   I fired across the river,
   Made water ripples shiver,
     And perhaps I killed a man
Upon that distant bank.

Who am I to play at fate,
To aim, and fire, and arbitrate
'Tween life and death; not knowing hate,
   To send with sad, departing whine
   Irrevocable death across the Rhine.
The willows answer not. The scent
Of clover lingered while I went
   Between the fields where ruins stand;
   Dead horses lie along the land,
   Who died, and did not understand
Why this should be; no more may I
Explain why any man should die.
And still I fired; and wonder why.

*Nijmegen, April 1945*
*Alexander McKee*

# Insensibility

### I

Happy are men who yet before they are killed
Can let their veins run cold.
Whom no compassion fleers
Or makes their feet
Sore on the alleys cobbled with their brothers.
The front line withers.
But they are troops who fade, not flowers,
For poets' tearful fooling:
Men, gaps for filling:
Losses, who might have fought
Longer; but no one bothers.

### II

And some cease feeling
Even themselves or for themselves.
Dullness best solves
The tease and doubt of shelling,
And Chance's strange arithmetic
Comes simpler than the reckoning of their shilling.
They keep no check on armies' decimation.

### III

Happy are these who lose imagination:
They have enough to carry with ammunition.
Their spirit drags no pack.
Their old wounds, save with cold, can not more ache.
Having seen all things red,
Their eyes are rid
Of the hurt of the colour of blood for ever.
And terror's first constriction over,
Their hearts remain small-drawn.
Their senses in some scorching cautery of battle
Now long since ironed,
Can laugh among the dying, unconcerned.

### IV

Happy the soldier home, with not a notion
How somewhere, every dawn, some men attack,
And many sighs are drained.
Happy the lad whose mind was never trained:
His days are worth forgetting more than not.
He sings along the march
Which we march taciturn, because of dusk,
The long, forlorn, relentless trend
From larger day to huger night.

### V

We wise, who with a thought besmirch
Blood over all our soul,
Hów should we see our task
But through his blunt and lashless eyes?
Alive, he is not vital overmuch;
Dying, not mortal overmuch;
Nor sad, nor proud,
Nor curious at all.
He cannot tell
Old men's placidity from his.

### VI

But cursed are dullards whom no cannon stuns,
That they should be as stones.
Wretched are they, and mean
With paucity that never was simplicity.
By choice they made themselves immune
To pity and whatever moans in man
Before the last sea and the hapless stars;
Whatever mourns when many leave these shores;
Whatever shares
The eternal reciprocity of tears.

*Wilfred Owen*

# Drummer Hodge

### I

They throw in Drummer Hodge, to rest
　　Uncoffined—just as found:
His landmark is a kopje-crest
　　That breaks the veldt around;
And foreign constellations west
　　Each night above his mound.

### II

Young Hodge the Drummer never knew—
　　Fresh from his Wessex home—
The meaning of the broad Karoo,
　　The Bush, the dusty loam,
And why uprose to nightly view
　　Strange stars amid the gloom.

### III

Yet portion of that unknown plain
　　Will Hodge for ever be;
His homely Northern breast and brain
　　Grow to some Southern tree,
And strange-eyed constellations reign
　　His stars eternally.

*Thomas Hardy*

# Tommy

I went into a public-'ouse to get a pint o' beer,
The publican 'e up an' sez, 'We serve no red-coats here.'
The girls be'ind the bar they laughed an' giggled fit to die,
I outs into the street again an' to myself sez I:
  O it's Tommy this, an' Tommy that, an' 'Tommy, go away';
  But it's 'Thank you, Mister Atkins,' when the band
    begins to play—
  The band begins to play, my boys, the band begins to play,
  O it's 'Thank you, Mister Atkins,' when the band begins to play.

I went into a theatre as sober as could be,
They gave a drunk civilian room, but 'adn't none for me;
They sent me to the gallery or round the music-'alls;
But when it comes to fightin', Lord! they'll shove me in the stalls!
  For it's Tommy this, an' Tommy that, an' 'Tommy wait outside';
  But it's 'Special train for Atkins' when the trooper's on the tide—
  The troopship's on the tide, my boys, the troopship's on the tide,
  O it's 'Special train for Atkins' when the trooper's on the tide.

Yes, makin' mock o' uniforms that guard you while you sleep
Is cheaper than them uniforms, an' they're starvation
    cheap;
An' hustlin' drunken soldiers when they're goin' large a bit
Is five times better business than paradin' in full kit.
  Then it's Tommy this, an' Tommy that, an' 'Tommy,
    'ow's yer soul?'
  But it's 'Thin red line of 'eroes' when the drums begin to roll—
  The drums begin to roll, my boys, the drums begin to roll,
  O it's 'Thin red line of 'eroes' when the drums begin to roll.

We aren't no thin red 'eroes, nor we aren't no blackguards too,
But single men in barricks, most remarkable like you;
An' if sometimes our conduck isn't all your fancy paints,
Why, single men in barricks don't grow into plaster saints;

While it's Tommy this, an' Tommy that, an' 'Tommy,
    fall be'ind,'
But it's 'Please to walk in front, sir,' when there's trouble
    in the wind—
There's trouble in the wind, my boys, there's trouble in
    the wind,
O it's 'Please to walk in front, sir,' when there's trouble
    in the wind.

You talk o' better food for us, an' schools, an' fires, an' all:
We'll wait for extry rations if you treat us rational.
Don't mess about the cook-room slops, but prove it to our face
The Widow's Uniform is not the soldier-man's disgrace.
    For it's Tommy this, an' Tommy that, an' 'Chuck him
        out, the brute!'
    But it's 'Saviour of 'is country' when the guns begin to shoot;
    An' it's Tommy this, an' Tommy that, an' anything you please;
    An' Tommy ain't a bloomin' fool—you bet that Tommy sees!

*Rudyard Kipling*

# A.B.C. of a Naval Trainee

A is the anger we hide with some danger,
Keeping it down like the twentieth beer.
B is the boredom we feel in this bedlam.
C is the cautious and supervised cheer.

D is the tea dope and E English duping,
Too feeble for folly, too strong for revolt.
F is the adjective near every object,
The chief of desires for both genius and dolt.

G is the gun which can kill at, say, Greenwich
If fired at St Martin's, and H is our hate
Non-existent behind it wherever we wind it.
I is the image of common man's fate.

J is the Joan or the Jill or Joanna,
Appearing in dreams as a just missed train.
K is the kindness like Christmas tree candles,
Unexpected and grateful as poppies in grain.

L is the lung or the limb which in languor
Rests after work and will soon be exposed
To M which is murder, a world rather madder,
Where what we pretend now's as real as your nose.

N is the nightingale's song that we're noting
When the sky is a lucid darkening silk,
When the guns are at rest and the heart is a cancer
And our mouths make O at the moon of milk.

Then we remember, no longer a number,
We think of our duties as poets and men:
Beyond us lie Paris, Quebec, Rome, where diaries
Of millions record the same troubles and pain.

S is the silence for brooding on violence.
T is the toughness imparted to all.
U is the unit that never will clown it
Again as the lonely, the shy or the tall.

V is the vastness: as actor and witness
We doubled our role and stammer at first.
W is war to start off the quarries—
Our everyday hunger and everynight thirst.

X is the kiss or the unknown, the fissure
In misery stretching far back to the ape.
Y is the yearning for Eden returning;
Our ending, our Z and our only escape.

*Roy Fuller*


# Elegy for an 88 Gunner

Three weeks gone and the combatants gone,
returning over the nightmare ground
we found the place again and found
the soldier sprawling in the sun.

The frowning barrel of his gun
overshadows him. As we came on
that day, he hit my tank with one
like the entry of a demon.

And smiling in the gunpit spoil
is a picture of his girl
who has written: *Steffi, Vergissmeinicht.*
in a copybook Gothic script.

We see him almost with content,
abased and seeming to have paid,
mocked by his durable equipment
that's hard and good when he's decayed.

But she would weep to see today
how on his skin the swart flies move,
the dust upon the paper eye
and the burst stomach like a cave.

For here the lover and the killer are mingled
who had one body and one heart;
and Death, who had the soldier singled
has done the lover mortal hurt.

*Homs, Tripolitania, 1943*
*Keith Douglas*


# 'Love Letters of the Dead'
## *A Commando Intelligence Briefing*

'Go through the pockets of the enemy wounded,
Go through the pockets of the enemy dead—
There's a lot of good stuff to be found there—
That's of course if you've time', I said.
'Love letters are specially useful,
It's amazing what couples let slip—
Effects of our bombs for example,
The size and type of a ship.
These'll all give us bits of our jigsaw.
Any questions?' I asked as per rule-book;
A close-cropped sergeant from Glasgow,
With an obstinate jut to his jaw,
Got up, and at me he pointed;
Then very slowly he said:
'Do you think it right, well I don't,
For any bloody stranger to snitch
What's special and sacred and secret,
Love letters of the dead?'

*Commando H.Q., December 1941*
*Douglas Street*

# What Were They Like?

1) Did the people of Vietnam
   use lanterns of stone?
2) Did they hold ceremonies
   to reverence the opening of buds?
3) Were they inclined to quiet laughter?
4) Did they use bone and ivory,
   jade and silver, for ornament?
5) Had they an epic poem?
6) Did they distinguish between speech and singing?

1) Sir, their light hearts turned to stone.
   It is not remembered whether in gardens
   stone lanterns illumined pleasant ways.
2) Perhaps they gathered once to delight in blossom,
   but after the children were killed
   there were no more buds.
3) Sir, laughter is bitter to the burned mouth.
4) A dream ago, perhaps. Ornament is for joy.
   All the bones were charred.
5) It is not remembered. Remember,
   most were peasants; their life
   was in rice and bamboo.
   When peaceful clouds were reflected in the paddies
   and the water buffalo stepped surely along terraces,
   maybe fathers told their sons old tales.
   When bombs smashed those mirrors
   there was time only to scream.
6) There is an echo yet
   of their speech which was like a song.
   It was reported their singing resembled
   the flight of moths in moonlight.
   Who can say? It is silent now.

*Denise Levertov*

# Does Spring Come to a Lost Land?

Now someone else's land . . . does Spring come to a
    usurped land?
Bathed all over in sunlight, I saunter as in a dream
Along the straight paddy-field path
To where the blue sky and the green field meet.
Silent sky and field! I have not come here alone.
Did you lure me? Or did someone call?
Please answer, I implore.
The wind whispers in my ears,
Pulling my sleeves to urge me on.
The larks are laughing behind the clouds
Like maidens hidden in the grove.

Fertile wheat fields! the gentle rain that started
After midnight has made your hair glow like hemp.
My hair feels so light, too.
Let me rush ahead, though all alone.
The kind ditches around the dry paddy-fields
Are singing lullabies as to a suckling babe,
Dancing in glee all alone.

Butterflies, swallows! do not hurry.
I must say hello to the cockscomb village, too.
I want to see that field the nameless maiden used to weed.

Let me take a hoe in my hand.
I will tread this soil tender as a plump breast
Till my ankles ache. I want to shed much sweat.
My soul races, free and boundless
Like children by the river-side.
What are you looking for? Where are you going?
It's strange, please answer.

My whole body smells of fresh greens.
I walk all day long, limping between green laughter and
    green sorrow.
I must be under Spring's spell.

But now the land is another's.
And Spring will be usurped, too, I fear.

*Sang-hwa Lee*
*translated from the Korean by Chang-soo Koh*

## Early March

We did not expect this; we were not ready for this;—
To find the unpredicted spring
Sprung open like a broken trap. The sky
Unfolds like an arum leaf; the bare
Trees unfurl like fronds of fern;
The birds are scattered along the air;
Celandines and cresses prick pinpoints white and yellow,
And the snow is stripped from the fells.
We were not prepared for this. We knew
That the avalanche of war breaks boundaries like birches,
That terror bursts round our roofs; we were aware
Of the soft cough of death in the waiting lungs. But this
Has caught us half asleep. We had never thought of this.

*Norman Nicholson*

# Lessons of the War: II. Judging Distances

Not only how far away, but the way that you say it
Is very important. Perhaps you may never get
The knack of judging a distance, but at least you know
How to report on a landscape: the central sector,
The right of arc and that, which we had last Tuesday,
     And at least you know

That maps are of time, not place, so far as the army
Happens to be concerned—the reason being,
Is one which need not delay us. Again, you know
There are three kinds of tree, three only, the fir and the poplar,
And those which have bushy tops to; and lastly
     That things only seem to be things.

A barn is not called a barn, to put it more plainly,
Or a field in the distance, where sheep may be safely grazing.
You must never be over-sure. You must say, when reporting:
At five o'clock in the central sector is a dozen
Of what appear to be animals; whatever you do,
     Don't call the bleeders *sheep*.

I am sure that's quite clear; and suppose, for the sake of example,
The one at the end, asleep, endeavours to tell us
What he sees over there to the west, and how far away,
After first having come to attention. There to the west,
On the fields of summer the sun and the shadows bestow
     Vestments of purple and gold.

The still white dwellings are like a mirage in the heat,
And under the swaying elms a man and a woman
Lie gently together. Which is, perhaps, only to say
That there is a row of houses to the left of arc,
And that under some poplars a pair of what appear to be humans
     Appear to be loving.

Well that, for an answer, is what we might rightly call
Moderately satisfactory only, the reason being,
Is that two things have been omitted, and those are important.

The human beings, now: in what direction are they,
And how far away, would you say? And do not forget
　　　There may be dead ground in between.

There may be dead ground in between; and I may not have got
The knack of judging a distance; I will only venture
A guess that perhaps between me and the apparent lovers,
(Who, incidentally, appear by now to have finished,)
At seven o'clock from the houses, is roughly a distance
　　　Of about one year and a half.

*Henry Reed*


# At the Bomb Testing Site

At noon in the desert a panting lizard
waited for history, its elbows tense,
watching the curve of a particular road
as if something might happen.

It was looking at something farther off
than people could see, an important scene
acted in stone for little selves
at the flute end of consequences.

There was just a continent without much on it
under a sky that never cared less.
Ready for a change, the elbows waited,
the hands gripped hard on the desert.

*William Stafford*

# Beat! Beat! Drums!

Beat! beat! drums!—blow! bugles! blow!
Through the windows—through doors—burst like a
    ruthless force,
Into the solemn church, and scatter the congregation,
Into the school where the scholar is studying;
Leave not the bridegroom quiet—no happiness must he
    have now with his bride.
Nor the peaceful farmer any peace, ploughing his field or
    gathering his grain,
So fierce you whirr and pound you drums—so shrill you
    bugles blow.

Beat! beat! drums!—blow! bugles! blow!
Over the traffic of cities—over the rumble of wheels in the streets;
Are beds prepared for sleepers at night in the houses? no sleepers
    must sleep in those beds,
No bargainers' bargains by day—no brokers or
    speculators—would they continue?
Would the talkers be talking? would the singer attempt to sing?
Would the lawyer rise in the court to state his case before
    the judge?
Then rattle quicker, heavier drums—you bugles wilder blow.

Beat! beat! drums!—blow! bugles! blow!
Make no parley—stop for no expostulation,
Mind not the timid—mind not the weeper or prayer,
Mind not the old man beseeching the young man,
Let not the child's voice be heard, nor the mother's entreaties,
Make even the trestles to shake the dead where they lie
    awaiting the hearses,
So strong you thump O terrible drums—so loud you bugles blow.

*Walt Whitman*

# The Drum

I hate that drum's discordant sound,
Parading round, and round, and round:
To thoughtless youth it pleasure yields,
And lures from cities and from fields,
To sell their liberty for charms
Of tawdry lace, and glittering arms;
And when Ambition's voice commands,
To march, and fight, and fall, in foreign lands.

I hate that drum's discordant sound,
Parading round, and round, and round:
To me it talks of ravaged plains,
And burning towns, and ruined swains,
And mangled limbs, and dying groans,
And widows' tears, and orphans' moans;
And all that Misery's hand bestows,
To fill the catalogue of human woes.

*John Scott of Amwell*


# The Long War

Less passionate the long war throws
its burning thorn about all men,
caught in one grief, we share one wound,
and cry one dialect of pain.

We have forgot who fired the house,
whose easy mischief spilt first blood,
under one raging roof we lie
the fault no longer understood.

But as our twisted arms embrace
the desert where our cities stood,
death's family likeness in each face
must show, at last, our brotherhood.

*Laurie Lee*

# 'From Many a Mangled Truth a War is Won'

From many a mangled truth a war is won
   And who am I to oppose
   War and the lie and the pose
Asserting a lie is good if a war be won?

From many a mangled truth a war is won
   And many a truth has died
   That has lived undenied
For always there must be loss that a war be won.

From many a mangled truth a war is won
   And when no thought is pure
   Who of us can be sure
Of lie and truth and war when the war is won?

*Clifford Dyment*


# War is Kind

Do not weep, maiden, for war is kind.
Because your lover threw wild hands toward the sky
And the affrighted steed ran on alone,
Do not weep.
War is kind.

   Hoarse, booming drums of the regiment,
   Little souls who thirst for fight,
   These men were born to drill and die.
   The unexplained glory flies above them,
   Great is the battle god, great, and his kingdom
   A field where a thousand corpses lie.

Do not weep, babe, for war is kind.
Because your father tumbled in the yellow trenches,
Raged at his breast, gulped and died,
Do not weep.
War is kind.

Swift blazing flag of the regiment,
Eagle with crest of red and gold,
These men were born to drill and die.
Point for them the virtue of slaughter,
Make plain to them the excellence of killing
And a field where a thousand corpses lie.

Mother whose heart hung humble as a button
On the bright splendid shroud of your son,
Do not weep,
War is kind.

*Stephen Crane*


# Sonnet 25

Let those who are in favour with their stars
Of public honour and proud titles boast,
Whilst I, whom fortune of such triumph bars
Unlook'd for joy in that I honour most.
Great princes' favourites their fair leaves spread
But as the marigold at the sun's eye,
And in themselves their pride lies buried,
For at a frown they in their glory die.
The painful warrior famoused for fight,
After a thousand victories once foil'd
Is from the book of honour razed quite,
And all the rest forgot for which he toil'd:
    Then happy I, that love and am beloved
    Where I may not remove nor be removed.

*William Shakespeare*

# Epitaph on an Army of Mercenaries

These, in the day when heaven was falling,
    The hour when earth's foundations fled,
Followed their mercenary calling
    And took their wages and are dead.

Their shoulders held the sky suspended;
    They stood, and earth's foundations stay;
What God abandoned, these defended,
    And saved the sum of things for pay.

*A. E. Housman*


# Another Epitaph on an Army of Mercenaries

It is a God-damned lie to say that these
Saved, or knew, anything worth any man's pride,
They were professional murderers and they took
Their blood money and impious risks and died.
In spite of all their kind some elements of worth
With difficulty persist here and there on earth.

*Hugh Macdiarmid*
*In reply to A. E. Housman*

# Epitaph on a New Army

No drums they wished, whose thoughts were tied
To girls and jobs and mother,
Who rose and drilled and killed and died
Because they saw no other,

Who died without the hero's throb,
And if they trembled, hid it,
Who did not fancy much their job
But thought it best, and did it.

*November 1939*
*Michael Thwaites*

# The Send-Off

Down the close, darkening lanes they sang their way
To the siding-shed,
And lined the train with faces grimly gay.

Their breasts were stuck all white with wreath and spray
As men's are, dead.

Dull porters watched them, and a casual tramp
Stood staring hard,
Sorry to miss them from the upland camp.
Then, unmoved, signals nodded, and a lamp
Winked to the guard.

So secretly, like wrongs hushed-up, they went.
They were not ours:
We never heard to which front these were sent.

Nor there if they yet mock what women meant
Who gave them flowers.

Shall they return to beatings of great bells
In wild train-loads?
A few, a few, too few for drums and yells,
May creep back, silent, to still village wells
Up half-known roads.

*Wilfred Owen*


# Gun Teams
## (Loos, September 1915)

Their rugs are sodden, their heads are down, their tails are
     turned to the storm:
(Would you know them, you who groomed them in the
     sleek fat days of peace,
When the tiles rang to their pawings in the lighted stalls,
     and warm,
Now the foul clay cakes on breeching strap and clogs the
     quick-release?)

The blown rain stings; there is never a star; the tracks are
     rivers of slime:
(You must harness-up by guesswork with a failing torch
     for light,
Instep-deep in unmade standings; for it's active-service time,
And our resting weeks are over, and we move the guns to-night.)

The tyres slither; the traces sag; their blind hoofs stumble
     and slide;
They are war-worn, they are weary, soaked with sweat
     and sopped with rain:
(You must hold them, you must help them, swing your
     lead and centre wide,
Where the greasy granite *pavé* peters out to squelching drain.)

There is shrapnel bursting a mile in front on the road that
     the guns must take:

(You are thoughtful, you are nervous, you are shifting in
    your seat,
As you watch the ragged feathers flicker orange, flame and break):
But the teams are pulling steady down the battered village street.

You have shod them cold, and their coats are long, and
    their bellies stiff with the mud;
They have done with gloss and polish, but the fighting
    heart's unbroke . . .
We, who saw them hobbling after us down white roads
    patched with blood.
Patient, wondering why we left them, till we lost them in
    the smoke;

Who have felt them shiver between our knees, when the
    shells rain black from the skies,
When the bursting terrors find us and the lines stampede as one;
Who have watched the pierced limbs quiver and the pain
    in stricken eyes;
Know the worth of humble servants, foolish-faithful to
    their gun.

*Gilbert Frankau*

# Destroyers in the Arctic

Camouflaged, they detach lengths of sea and sky
When they move; offset, speed and direction are a lie.

Everything is grey anyway; ships, water, snow, faces.
Flanking the convoy, we rarely go through our paces:

But sometimes on tightening waves at night they wheel
Drawing white moons on strings from dripping keel.

Cold cases them, like ships in glass; they are formal,
Not real, except in adversity. Then, too, have to seem normal.

At dusk they intensify, strung out, non-committal:
Waves spill from our wake, crêpe paper magnetized by gun metal.

They breathe silence, less solid than ghosts, ruminative
As the Arctic breaks up on their sides and they sieve

Moisture into mess-decks. Heat is cold-lined there,
Where we wait for a torpedo and lack air.

Repetitive of each other, imitating the sea's lift and fall,
On the wings of the convoy they indicate rehearsal.

Merchantmen move sideways, with the gait of crustaceans,
Round whom like eels escorts take up their stations.

Landfall, Murmansk; but starboard now a lead-coloured
Island, Jan Mayen. Days identical, hoisted like sails, blurred.

Counters moved on an Admiralty map, snow like confetti
Covers the real us. We dream we are counterfeits tied to our jetty.

But cannot dream long; the sea curdles and sprawls,
Liverishly real, and merciless all else away from us falls.

*Alan Ross*

# To a Home-town Conscript Posted Overseas

Just the right age to take an interest in the job
We marched rebellious from our mothers' parlours,
Stuffed with our fathers' pride, and wild
To be told they'd make us into fighting men.
Remember when the train clocked in, the laughter
Of the boys above the noise of arriving, the talk
Of brown-limbed women waiting in foreign ports.

Who, as far as I know, are waiting still, unless
You found them there—ready to drown your dreams
Deep in their deep black hair. Did you learn
To love and kill with equal ease, lost
In that flag-strung corner of the shrinking globe
Where neither common bond nor grief dare meddle
With that brief display of duty and its wake's despair?

And what of those we left there? Do their names,
On brass plaques, strengthen the sacrificial myth
Or fill out history in home-town museums?
With us, they felt the long nights soak
Like black-lead through their bones; alone,
Would uncrease last week's mail, or tick away
The calendar that should have brought them home.

*Peter Bland*

# Where are the War Poets?

They who in folly or mere greed
Enslaved religion, markets, laws,
Borrow our language now and bid
Us to speak up in freedom's cause.

It is the logic of our times,
No subject for immortal verse—
That we who lived by honest dreams
Defend the bad against the worse.

*C. Day Lewis*


# War Poet

I am the man who looked for peace and found
My own eyes barbed.
I am the man who groped for words and found
An arrow in my hand.
I am the builder whose firm walls surround
A slipping land.
When I grow sick or mad
Mock me not nor chain me:
When I reach for the wind
Cast me not down:
Though my face is a burnt book
And a wasted town.

*Sidney Keyes*

# On Being Asked for a War Poem

I think it better that in times like these
A poet's mouth be silent, for in truth
We have no gift to set a statesman right;
He has had enough of meddling who can please
A young girl in the indolence of her youth,
Or an old man upon a winter's night.

*W. B. Yeats*

# War Poet

We in our haste can only see the small components of the scene;
We cannot tell what incidents will focus on the final screen.
A barrage of disruptive sound, a petal on a sleeping face,
Both must be noted, both must have their place;

It may be that our later selves or else our unborn sons
Will search for meaning in the dust of long deserted guns,
We only watch, and indicate and make our scribbled
        pencil notes.
We do not wish to moralize, only to ease our dusty throats.

*Donald Bain*

# Poem in 1944

No, I cannot write the poem of war,
Neither the colossal dying nor the local scene,
A platoon asleep and dreaming of girls' warmth
Or by the petrol-cooker scraping out a laughter.
—Only the images that are not even nightmare:
A globe encrusted with a skin or seaweed,
Or razors at the roots. The heart is no man's prism
To cast a frozen shadow down the streaming future;
At most a cold slipstream of empty sorrow,
The grapes and melody of a dreamed love
Or a vague roar of courage.

           No. I am not
The meeting point of event and vision, where the poem
Bursts into flame, and the heart's engine
Takes on the load of these broken years and lifts it.
I am not even the tongue and the hand that write
The dissolving sweetness of a personal view
Like those who now in greater luck and liberty
Are professionally pitiful or heroic . . .

Into what eye to imagine the vista pouring
Its violent treasures? For I must believe
That somewhere the poet is working who can handle
The flung world and his own heart. To him I say
The little I can. I offer him the debris
Of five years undirected storm in self and Europe,
And my love. Let him take it for what it's worth
In this poem scarcely made and already forgotten.

*Robert Conquest*

# I Saw a Broken Town

I saw a broken town beside the grey March sea,
Spray flung in the air and no larks singing,
And houses lurching, twisted, where the chestnut trees
Stand ripped and stark; the fierce wind bringing
The choking dust in clouds along deserted streets,
Shaking the gaping rooms, the jagged, raw-white stone.
Seeking for what in this quiet, stricken town? It beats
About each fallen wall, each beam, leaving no livid,
        aching place alone.

*March 1941, after the bombing of Wallasey*
*Mabel Esther Allan*

# The Black-Out

I never feared the darkness as a child,
For then night's plumy wings that wrapped me round
Seemed gentle, and all earthly sound,
Whether man's movement or the wild,
Small stirrings of the beasts and trees, was kind,
So I was well contented to be blind.

But now the darkness is a time of dread,
Of stumbling, fearful progress, when one thinks,
With angry fear, that those dull amber chinks,
Which tell of life where all things else seem dead,
Are full of menace as a tiger's eyes
That watch our passing, hungry for the prize.

Over all Europe lies this shuddering night.
Sometimes it quivers like a beast of prey,
All tense to spring, or, trembling, turns at bay
Knowing itself too weak for force or flight,
And in all towns men strain their eyes and ears,
Like hunted beasts, for warning of their fears.

*Mary Desirée Anderson*

# Achtung! Achtung!

I'm war. Remember me?
'Yes, you're asleep,' you say, 'and you kill men,'
Look in my game-bag, fuller than you think.

I kill marriages.
If one dies, one weeps and then heals clean.
(No scar without infection.) That's no good.
I can do better when I really try.
I wear down the good small faiths, enough
For little strains of peace, the near, the known,
But not for the big absence, man-sized silences,
Family pack of dangers, primate lusts
I hang on them.

I kill families.
Cut off the roots, the plant will root no more.
Tossed from thin kindness to thin kindness on
The child grows no more love; will only seek
A pinchbeck eros and a tawdry shock.
I teach the race to dread its unborn freak.
I maim well.

I drink gold.
How kind of you to pour it without stint
Into my sleeping throat. In case I die?
You think I'm god, the one that pours the most
Getting my sanction? Well, perhaps you're right.
Divert it, anyway, from the use of peace;
Keep the gross gaol, starvation and the lout,
The succulent tumour, loving bacillus, the clot
As bright as mine, friends all. I pop their prey
Into my bag.

I am the game that nobody can win.
What's yours is mine, what's mine is still my own.
I'm War. Remember me.

*Mary Hacker*

# Troy

I keep the gate. Others ride out,
sally, retreat, but the plain offers
nothing but rock and dust, no escape.

Walls the gods made stand stripped
of bright banners. Our trophies rust.
Victories mock us. I have dreamed

of green islands, peace havened
and anchored. But war possesses us.
Helen keeps her room, lives in her mirror.

We can scarcely remember her fluttering
silks in the palace walks, a peacock
beside her. Hector in his cups

betters old battles. And always new heroes
go trotting past, armour like fire,
act out their loud drama.

But the foe is implacable.
Alert in darkness, his fires watch us.
We peer from the parapet

for dawn's insidious attack, knowing
the walls will be breached, towers fall.
I sit at the gate. The day yawns.

Fixed on stone a lizard stares.
I have been one in the throng
that marches, makes a division, mans a battle.

And so long at it. I haunt my past,
search for a single glorious act
I could unfurl to ride out under,

before the walls fall. I should welcome
some sign from the gods: a gift.

*Paul Coltman*

# A Moment of War

It is night like a red rag
drawn across the eyes

the flesh is bitterly pinned
to desperate vigilance

the blood is stuttering with fear

*O praise the security of worms*
*in cool crumbs of soil,*
*flatter the hidden sap*
*and the lost unfertilized spawn of fish!*

The hands melt with weakness
into the gun's hot iron

the body melts with pity,

the face is braced for wounds
the odour and the kiss of final pain.

*O envy the peace of women*
*giving birth and love like toys*
*into the hands of men!*

The mouth chatters with pale curses

the bowels struggle like a nest of rats

the feet wish they were grass
spaced quietly.

*O Christ and Mother!*

But darkness opens like a knife for you
and you are marked down by your pulsing brain

and isolated

and your breathing,

your breathing is the blast, the bullet,
and the final sky.

*Spanish Frontier, 1937*
*Laurie Lee*

## August 1914

What in our lives is burnt
In the fire of this?
The heart's dear granary?
The much we shall miss?

Three lives hath one life—
Iron, honey, gold.
The gold, the honey gone—
Left is the hard and cold.

Iron are our lives
Molten right through our youth.
A burnt space through ripe fields,
A fair mouth's broken tooth.

*Isaac Rosenberg*

# Break of Day in the Trenches

The darkness crumbles away.
It is the same old druid Time as ever,
Only a live thing leaps my hand,
A queer sardonic rat,
As I pull the parapet's poppy
To stick behind my ear.
Droll rat, they would shoot you if they knew
Your cosmopolitan sympathies.
Now you have touched this English hand
You will do the same to a German
Soon, no doubt, if it be your pleasure
To cross the sleeping green between.
It seems you inwardly grin as you pass
Strong eyes, fine limbs, haughty athletes,
Less chanced than you for life,
Bonds to the whims of murder,
Sprawled in the bowels of the earth,
The torn fields of France.
What do you see in our eyes
At the shrieking iron and flame
Hurled through still heavens?
What quaver—what heart aghast?
Poppies whose roots are in man's veins
Drop, and are ever dropping;
But mine in my ear is safe—
Just a little white with the dust.

*Isaac Rosenberg*

# Exposure

Our brains ache, in the merciless iced east winds that knive us . . .
Wearied we keep awake because the night is silent . . .
Low, drooping flares confuse our memory of the salient . . .
Worried by silence, sentries whisper, curious, nervous,
    But nothing happens.

Watching, we hear the mad gusts tugging on the wire,
Like twitching agonies of men among its brambles.
Northward, incessantly, the flickering gunnery rumbles,
Far off, like a dull rumour of some other war.
    What are we doing here?

The poignant misery of dawn begins to grow . . .
We only know war lasts, rain soaks, and clouds sag stormy.
Dawn massing in the east her melancholy army
Attacks once more in ranks on shivering ranks of grey,
    But nothing happens.

Sudden successive flights of bullets streak the silence.
Less deathly than the air that shudders black with snow,
With sidelong flowing flakes that flock, pause, and renew;
We watch them wandering up and down the wind's nonchalance,
    But nothing happens.

Pale flakes with fingering stealth come feeling for our faces—
We cringe in holes, back on forgotten dreams, and stare, snow-dazed,
Deep into grassier ditches. So we drowse, sun-dozed,
Littered with blossoms trickling where the blackbird fusses,
    —Is it that we are dying?

Slowly our ghosts drag home: glimpsing the sunk fires, glozed
With crusted dark-red jewels; crickets jingle there;
For hours the innocent mice rejoice: the house is theirs;
Shutters and doors, all closed: on us the doors are closed,—
    We turn back to our dying.

Since we believe not otherwise can kind fires burn;
Nor ever suns smile true on child, or field, or fruit.
For God's invincible spring our love is made afraid;
Therefore, not loath, we lie out here; therefore were born,
    For love of God seems dying.

Tonight, this frost will fasten on this mud and us,
Shrivelling many hands, puckering foreheads crisp.
The burying-party, picks and shovels in shaking grasp,
Pause over half-known faces. All their eyes are ice,
    But nothing happens.

*Wilfred Owen*

The word was given, and, instantaneously,
Oars smote the roaring waves in unison
And churned the foam up. Soon their whole fleet appeared;
The port division thrown out like a horn
In precise order; then the main of them
Put out against us. We could plainly hear
The thunder of their shouting as they came.
'Forth, sons of Hellas! free your land, and free
Your children and your wives, the native seats
Of Gods your fathers worshipped and their graves.
This is a bout that hazards all ye have.'
And verily from us in the Persian tongue
There rose an answering roar; the long suspense

Was ended. In an instant, ship smote ship,
With thrust of armoured prow. The first to ram
Was a Greek; that impact carried clean away
A tall Phoenician's poop. Then all came on,
Each steering forthright for a ship of ours.
At first the encountering tide of Persians held;
But caught in the narrows, crowded without sea-room,
None could help other; nay, they fell aboard
Their own ships, crashing in with beak of bronze,
Till all their oars were smashed. But the Hellenes
Rowed round and round, and with sure seamanship
Struck where they chose. Many of ours capsized,
Until the very sea was hid from sight
Choked up with drifting wreckage and drowning men.
The beaches and low rocks were stacked with corpses:
The few barbarian vessels still afloat,
Fouling each other fled in headlong rout.
But they with broken oars and splintered spars
Beat us like tunnies or a draught of fish,
Yea, smote men's backs asunder; and all the while
Shrieking and wailing hushed the ocean surge,
Till night looked down and they were rapt away.
But, truly, if I should discourse the length
Of ten long days I could not sum our woes.
There never yet 'twixt sunrise and sunset
Perished so vast a multitude of men.

*Aeschylus, The Persians*
*translated from the Ancient Greek by G. M. Cookson*

# Hohenlinden

On Linden, when the sun was low,
All bloodless lay the untrodden snow,
And dark as winter was the flow
   Of Iser, rolling rapidly.

But Linden saw another sight,
When the drum beat, at dead of night,
Commanding fires of death to light
   The darkness of her scenery.

By torch and trumpet fast arrayed,
Each horseman drew his battle blade,
And furious every charger neighed
   To join the dreadful revelry.

Then shook the hills, with thunder riven;
Then rushed the steed, to battle driven;
And, louder than the bolts of heaven,
   Far flashed the red artillery.

But redder yet that light shall glow,
On Linden's hills of stainèd snow;
And bloodier yet, the torrent flow
   Of Iser, rolling rapidly.

'Tis morn; but scarce yon level sun
Can pierce the war-clouds, rolling dun,
Where furious Frank, and fiery Hun,
   Shout in their sulphurous canopy.

The combat deepens. On, ye brave,
Who rush to glory, or the grave!
Wave, Munich, all thy banners wave,
   And charge with all thy chivalry!

Few, few shall part, where many meet!
The snow shall be their winding sheet,
And every turf, beneath their feet,
   Shall be a soldier's sepulchre.

*Thomas Campbell*

# The Legend of the Dead Soldier

*(from the German of Bertolt Brecht)*

And as the war in its fifth spring
Gave no inkling of peace,
The soldier drew the logical conclusion
And died a hero's death.

But the war was not yet over,
And therefore the Kaiser was vexed
That his soldier had died so soon,
It struck him as premature.

The summer crept over the graves
And the soldier was already asleep.
Then came along one night a Mil-
itary Medical Mission Extraordinary.

The Medical Mission proceeded
To visit God's Own Acre,
And with consecrated spades they ex-
cavated the fallen soldier.

The doctor overhauled him thoroughly—
Or rather, that is, what was left of him—
And the doctor found that the soldier was O.K.,
His injuries being occupational.

And at once they abducted the soldier.
The night was blue and beautiful:
Anyone who took his tin hat off
Could have seen the stars of home.

And because the soldier stinks of decay
A priest hobbles in front
Who swings a censer above
In order to stop him stinking.

Ahead the band with tow-row-row
Plays a rollicking march,
And the soldier, in accordance with instructions,
Goosesteps high from his arse.

And brotherly-wise two medical
Orderlies hold him up;
Otherwise he would collapse in the mud—
And that is strictly forbidden.

They painted his winding sheet with the three
Colours—the black-white-red—
And carried it before him; the colours
Prevented one seeing the filth.

A gentleman in morning dress,
Equipped with an athlete's chest,
Led the way; as a German
He was quite *au fait* with his duty.

So they took him, playing a tow-row-row,
Down the dark arterial road,
And the soldier staggered along
Like a flake of snow in a storm.

And as they passed through the villages
All the women were there.
The trees made a bow, the full moon shone,
And every one cried 'Hurrah'.

With a tow-row-row and welcome home!
And woman, dog and priest!
And right in the middle the dead soldier
Drunk as a drunken ape.

And as they passed through the villages
No one was able to see him;
You could only have seen him from above—
And up there is nothing but stars.

The stars are not always there,
The red dawn is a-dawning.
But the soldier, in accordance with instructions,
Goes to a hero's grave.

*Louis MacNeice*

# David's Lament over Saul

The beauty of Israel is slain upon thy high places:
> how are the mighty fallen!

Tell it not in Gath, publish it not in the streets of Askelon;
> lest the daughters of the Philistines rejoice,
> lest the daughters of the uncircumcised triumph.

Ye mountains of Gilboa, let there be no dew,
> neither let there be rain upon you,
> nor fields of offerings:
> for there the shield of the mighty is vilely cast away,
> the shield of Saul, as though he had not been anointed
> with oil.

From the blood of the slain, from the fat of the mighty,
> the bow of Jonathan turned not back,
> and the sword of Saul returned not empty.

Saul and Jonathan were lovely and pleasant in their lives,
> and in their death they were not divided;

they were swifter than eagles, they were stronger than
> lions.

Ye daughters of Israel, weep over Saul, who clothed you in
> scarlet, with other delights, who put on ornaments of
> gold
> upon your apparel.

How are the mighty fallen in the midst of the battle!

O Jonathan, thou wast slain in thine high places.

I am distressed for thee, my brother Jonathan:
> very pleasant hast thou been unto me:
> thy love to me was wonderful, passing the love of
> women.

How are the mighty fallen, and the weapons of war
> perished!

*II Samuel I : 19–27*
*The Bible: King James Version*

# Six Young Men

The celluloid of a photograph holds them well—
Six young men, familiar to their friends.
Four decades that have faded and ochre-tinged
This photograph have not wrinkled the faces or the hands.
Though their cocked hats are not now fashionable,
Their shoes shine. One imparts an intimate smile,
One chews a grass, one lowers his eyes, bashful,
One is ridiculous with cocky pride—
Six months after this picture they were all dead.

All are trimmed for a Sunday jaunt. I know
That bilberried bank, that thick tree, that black wall,
Which are there yet and not changed. From where these sit
You hear the water of seven streams fall
To the roarer in the bottom, and through all
The leafy valley a rumouring of air go.
Pictured here, their expressions listen yet,
And still that valley has not changed its sound
Though their faces are four decades under the ground.

This one was shot in an attack and lay
Calling in the wire, then this one, his best friend,
Went out to bring him in and was shot too;
And this one, the very moment he was warned
From potting at tin-cans in no-man's-land,
Fell back dead with his rifle-sights shot away.
The rest, nobody knows what they came to,
But come to the worst they must have done, and held it
Closer than their hope; all were killed.

Here see a man's photograph,
The locket of a smile, turned overnight
Into the hospital of his mangled last
Agony and hours; see bundled in it
His mightier-than-a-man dead bulk and weight:
And on this one place which keeps him alive
(In his Sunday best) see fall war's worst
Thinkable flash and rending, onto his smile
Forty years rotting into soil.

That man's not more alive whom you confront
And shake by the hand, see hale, hear speak loud,
Than any of these six celluloid smiles are,
Nor prehistoric or fabulous beast more dead;
No thought so vivid as their smoking blood:
To regard this photograph might well dement,
Such contradictory permanent horrors here
Smile from the single exposure and shoulder out
One's own body from its instant and heat.

*Ted Hughes*


## The Question

I wonder if the old cow died or not.
　　Gey bad she was the night I left, and sick.
Dick reckoned she would mend. He knows a lot—
　　At least he fancies so himself, does Dick.

Dick knows a lot. But maybe I did wrong
　　To leave the cow to him, and come away.
Over and over like a silly song
　　These words keep bumming in my head all day.

And all I think of, as I face the foe
　　And take my lucky chance of being shot,
Is this—that if I'm hit, I'll never know
　　Till Doomsday if the old cow died or not.

*Wilfrid Wilson Gibson*

# Suicide in the Trenches

I knew a simple soldier boy
Who grinned at life in empty joy,
Slept soundly through the lonesome dark,
And whistled early with the lark.

In winter trenches, cowed and glum,
With crumps and lice and lack of rum,
He put a bullet through his brain.
No one spoke of him again.

You smug-faced crowds with kindling eye
Who cheer when soldier lads march by,
Sneak home and pray you'll never know
The hell where youth and laughter go.

*Siegfried Sassoon*


# The Volunteer

Here lies a clerk who half his life had spent
Toiling at ledgers in a city grey,
Thinking that so his days would drift away
With no lance broken in life's tournament:
Yet ever 'twixt the books and his bright eyes
The gleaming eagles of the legions came,
And horsemen, charging under phantom skies,
Went thundering past beneath the oriflamme.

And now those waiting dreams are satisfied;
From twilight to the halls of dawn he went;
His lance is broken; but he lies content
With that high hour, in which he lived and died.
And falling thus, he wants no recompense,
Who found his battle in the last resort;
Nor needs he any hearse to bear him hence,
Who goes to join the men of Agincourt.

*Herbert Asquith*

# Luck

I suppose they'll say his last thoughts were of simple
    things,
Of April back at home, and the late sun on his wings;
Or that he murmured someone's name
As earth reclaimed him sheathed in flame.
Oh God! Let's have no more of empty words,
Lip service ornamenting death!
The worms don't spare the hero;
Nor can children feed upon resounding praises of his deed.
'He died who loved to live,' they'll say,
'Unselfishly so we might have today!'
Like hell! He fought because he had to fight;
He died that's all. It was his unlucky night.

*Dennis McHarrie*


# My Comrades

They were burnt in tanks, my comrades,
burnt to embers, cinders, reduced to ash.
Grass grew out of them, of course,
grass that spreads over half the world.
My comrades
         were blown up
on mines,
        pitched high in the air,
and many stars, remote and peaceful,
were kindled
        from them,
            from my friends.
There's talk of them on holidays,
they're shown on films,
and those who were my schoolmates and fellow students
have long since become lines in poems.

*Boris Slutsky*
*translated from the Russian by George Reavey*

# Waterloo

'Oh man, don't make a noise' the officer
Said kindly to the wounded soldier, who
Went quiet from then to death. Nobody knew
What the battle would be called, nor
Did it seem different from the day's before.
A tabby kitten from the nearby town
Lay killed. The mid-June wheat was trodden down
Smelling of itself and gunpowder.

Smoke stood between friend and friend and hid the weather.
Only the flaring of the guns picked out
The battlefield. The evening was victorious.
Sky and a kind of joy came back together.
Almost too late to show a lost and glorious
Summer day, the sun about to set.

*Patricia Beer*

# Lost in France
# Jo's Requiem

He had the plowman's strength
in the grasp of his hand:
He could see a crow
three miles away,
and the trout beneath the stone.
He could hear the green oats growing,
and the south-west wind making rain.
He could hear the wheel upon the hill
when it left the level road.
He could make a gate, and dig a pit,
And plow as straight as stone can fall.
And he is dead.

*Ernest Rhys*

# Survivors

With the ship burning in their eyes
The white faces float like refuse
In the darkness—the water screwing
Oily circles where the hot steel lies.

They clutch with fingers frozen into claws
The lifebelts thrown from a destroyer,
And see, between the future's doors,
The gasping entrance of the sea.

Taken on board as many as lived, who
Had a mind left for living and the ocean,
They open eyes running with surf,
Heavy with the grey ghosts of explosion.

The meaning is not yet clear,
Where daybreak died in the smile—
And the mouth remained stiff
And grinning, stupid for a while.

But soon they joke, easy and warm,
As men will who have died once
Yet somehow were able to find their way—
Muttering this was not included in their pay.

Later, sleepless at night, the brain spinning
With cracked images, they won't forget
The confusion and the oily dead,
Nor yet the casual knack of living.

*Alan Ross*

# The Man he Killed

'Had he and I but met
  By some old ancient inn,
We should have sat us down to wet
  Right many a nipperkin!

'But ranged as infantry,
  And staring face to face,
I shot at him as he at me,
  And killed him in his place.

'I shot him dead because—
  Because he was my foe,
Just so: my foe of course he was;
  That's clear enough: although

'He thought he'd 'list, perhaps,
  Off-hand like—just as I;
Was out of work, had sold his traps—
  No other reason why.

'Yes; quaint and curious war is!
  You shoot a fellow down
You'd treat if met where any bar is,
  Or help to half-a-crown.'

*Thomas Hardy*

# Reconciliation

Word over all, beautiful as the sky,
Beautiful that war and all its deeds of carnage must in time
    be utterly lost,
That the hands of the sisters Death and Night incessantly
    softly wash again, and ever again, this soiled world;
For my enemy is dead, a man divine as myself is dead,
I look where he lies white-faced and still in the coffin—I
    draw near,
Bend down, and touch lightly with my lips the white face
    in the coffin.

*Walt Whitman*


# Reason for Refusal

Busy old lady, charitable tray
Of social emblems: poppies, people's blood—
I must refuse, make you flush pink
Perplexed by abrupt No-thank-you.
Yearly I keep up this small priggishness,
Would wince worse if I wore one.
Make me feel better, fetch a white feather, do.

Everyone has list of dead in war,
Regrets most of them, e.g.

Uncle Cyril; small boy in lace and velvet
With pushing sisters muscling all around him,
And lofty brothers, whiskers and stiff collars;
The youngest was the one who copped it.
My mother showed him to me,
Neat letters high up on the cenotaph
That wedding-caked it up above the park,
And shadowed birds on Isaac Watts' white shoulders.

And father's friends, like Sandy Vincent;
Brushed sandy hair, moustache, and staring eyes.
Kitchener claimed him, but the Southern Railway
Held back my father, made him guilty.
I hated the khaki photograph,
It left a patch on the wallpaper after I took it down.

Others I knew stick in the mind,
And Tony Lister often—
Eyes like holes in foolscap, suffered from piles,
Day after day went sick with constipation
Until they told him he could drive a truck—
Blown up with Second Troop in Greece:

We sang all night once when we were on guard.
And Ken Gee, our lance-corporal, Christian Scientist—
Everyone liked him, knew that he was good—
Had leg and arm blown off, then died.

Not all were good. Gross Corporal Rowlandson
Fell in the canal, the corrupt Sweet-water,
And rolled there like a log, drunk and drowned.
And I've always been glad of the death of Dick Benjamin,
A foxy urgent dainty ball-room dancer—
Found a new role in military necessity
As R.S.M. He waltzed out on parade
To make himself hated. Really hated, not an act.
He was a proper little porcelain sergeant-major—
The earliest bomb made smithereens;
Coincidence only, several have assured me.

In the school hall was pretty glass
Where prissy light shone through St George—
The highest holiest manhood, he!
And underneath were slain Old Boys
In tasteful lettering on whited slab—
And, each November, Ferdy the Headmaster
Reared himself squat and rolled his eyeballs upward,
Rolled the whole roll-call off an oily tongue,
Remorselessly from A to Z.

Of all the squirmers, Roger Frampton's lips
Most elegantly curled, showed most disgust.
He was a pattern of accomplishments,
And joined the Party first, and left it first,
At OCTU won a prize belt, most improbable,
Was desert-killed in '40, much too soon.

His name should burn right through that monument.

No poppy, thank you.

*Martin Bell*


## Picture from the Blitz

After all these years
I can still close my eyes and see
her sitting there,
in her big armchair,
grotesque under an open sky,
framed by the jagged lines of her broken house.

Sitting there,
a plump homely person,
steel needles still in her work-rough hands;
grey with dust, stiff with shock,
but breathing,
no blood or distorted limbs;
breathing, but stiff with shock,
knitting unravelling on her apron'd knee.

They have taken the stretchers off my car
and I am running
under the pattering flack
over a mangled garden;
treading on something soft
and fighting the rising nausea—
only a far-flung cushion, bleeding feathers.

They lift her gently
out of her great armchair,
tenderly,
under the open sky,
a shock-frozen woman trailing khaki wool.

*Lois Clark*


# History Teacher in the Warsaw Ghetto Rising

The schoolmaster once known as
Umbrella Feet
unfolds his six foot length
of gangling bone

and, mild as usual,
blinks—his bi-focals
having gone the way of his pipe
and his tree-shaded study
and his wife Charlotte—

jacket flapping, as usual,
carpet slippers treading
rubble of smashed cellars,

holding his rifle uncertainly
as if he thought it irrelevant
—as indeed it is—

advances steadily into the
glare of the burning street

leading his scattered handful
of scarecrow twelve-year-olds

towards the last ten minutes
of their own brief history.

*Evangeline Paterson*

# A Refusal to Mourn the Death, by Fire, of a Child in London

Never until the mankind making
Bird beast and flower
Fathering and all humbling darkness
Tells with silence the last light breaking
And the still hour
Is come of the sea tumbling in harness

And I must enter again the round
Zion of the water bead
And the synagogue of the ear of corn
Shall I let pray the shadow of a sound
Or sow my salt seed
In the least valley of sackcloth to mourn.

The majesty and burning of the child's death.
I shall not murder
The mankind of her going with a grave truth
Nor blaspheme down the stations of the breath
With any further
Elegy of innocence and youth.

Deep with the first dead lies London's daughter,
Robed in the long friends,
The grains beyond age, the dark veins of her mother,
Secret by the unmourning water
Of the riding Thames.
After the first death, there is no other.

*Dylan Thomas*

# The Children

Upon the street they lie
Beside the broken stone:
The blood of children stares from the broken stone.

Death came out of the sky
In the bright afternoon:
Darkness slanted over the bright afternoon.

Again the sky is clear
But upon earth a stain:
The earth is darkened with a darkening stain:

A wound which everywhere
Corrupts the hearts of men:
The blood of children corrupts the hearts of men.

Silence is in the air:
The stars move to their places:
Silent and serene the stars move to their places:

But from the earth the children stare
With blind and fearful faces:
And our charity is in the children's faces.

*William Soutar*

## 'I Looked Up from My Writing'

I looked up from my writing,
   And gave a start to see,
As if rapt in my inditing,
   The moon's full gaze on me.

Her meditative misty head
   Was spectral in its air,
And I involuntarily said,
   'What are you doing there?'

'Oh, I've been scanning pond and hole
   And waterway hereabout
For the body of one with a sunken soul
   Who has put his life-light out.

'Did you hear his frenzied tattle?
    It was sorrow for his son
Who is slain in brutish battle,
    Though he has injured none.

'And now I am curious to look
    Into the blinkered mind
Of one who wants to write a book
    In a world of such a kind.'

Her temper overwrought me,
    And I edged to shun her view,
For I felt assured she thought me
    One who should drown him too.

*Thomas Hardy*

Oh stay at home, my lad, and plough
   The land and not the sea,
And leave the soldiers at their drill,
And all about the idle hill
   Shepherd your sheep with me.

Oh stay with company and mirth
   And daylight and the air;
Too full already is the grave
Of fellows that were good and brave
   And died because they were.

*A. E. Housman*

## He Died Smiling

Patting goodbye, his father said, 'My lad,
   You'll always show the Hun a brave man's face.
   I'd rather you were dead than in disgrace.
We're proud to see you going, Jim, we're glad.'

His mother whimpered, 'Jim, my boy, I frets
   Until ye git a nice safe wound, I do.'
   His sisters said: why couldn't they go too.
His brothers said they'd send him cigarettes.

For three years, once a week, they wrote the same,
   Adding, 'We hope you use the Y. M. Hut.'
   And once a day came twenty Navy Cut.
And once an hour a bullet missed its aim.

And misses teased the hunger of his brain.
   His eyes grew scorched with wincing, and his hand
   Reckless with ague. Courage leaked, like sand
From sandbags that have stood three years of rain.

*Wilfred Owen*

# Don't Believe in War

Don't believe in war, my boy,
don't believe, it's quite depressing,
it's as depressing, boy,
as a pair of boots that pinch.

Those swift romantic steeds of yours,
they are good for nothing here;
you're as exposed as an open palm,
and the bullets' only target.

*Bulat Okudzhava*
*translated from the Russian by George Reavey*


# The Enemy

The moon had a courtyard
into which they shoved cannons.
The sun had a light
of which they made torches.
The field was filled with corn
of which they made scrap.

The night had a coat
from which they cut camouflage.
The man had a fist
of which they made bombs.
The woman had a lap
which they named a tavern.

The children had clear vision
they knew their enemy
and made use of everything.

*Bettina Wegner*
*translated from the German by Agnes Stein*

# The Kite

Over the empty fields a black kite hovers,
    And circle after circle smoothly weaves.
In the poor hut, over her son in the cradle
    A mother grieves:
'There, suck my breast: there grow and take our bread,
And learn to bear your cross and bow your head.'

Time passes. War returns. Rebellion rages.
    The farms and villages go up in flame,
And Russia in her ancient tear-stained beauty,
    Is yet the same,
Unchanged through all the ages. How long will
The mother grieve and the kite circle still?

*Alexander Blok*
*translated from the Russian by Frances Cornford*
*and Esther Polianowsky Salamon*

# A War Film

I saw,
With a catch of the breath and the heart's uplifting,
Sorrow and pride,
    The 'week's great draw'—
The Mons Retreat;
The 'Old Contemptibles' who fought, and died,
The horror and the anguish and the glory.

As in a dream,
Still hearing machine-guns rattle and shells scream,
I came out into the street.

When the day was done,
My little son
Wondered at bath-time why I kissed him so,
Naked upon my knee.
How could he know

The sudden terror that assaulted me? . . .
The body I had borne
Nine moons beneath my heart,
A part of me . . .
If, someday,
It should be taken away
To War. Tortured. Torn.
Slain.
Rotting in No Man's Land, out in the rain—
My little son . . .
Yet all those men had mothers, every one.

How should he know
Why I kissed and kissed and kissed him, crooning his
  name?
He thought that I was daft.
He thought it was a game,
And laughed, and laughed.

*Teresa Hooley*


# War and Hell

There is 'great rejoicing at the nation's capital'. So says the
  morning's paper.
The enemy's fleet has been annihilated.
Mothers are delighted because other mothers have lost sons
  just like their own;
Wives and daughters smile at the thought of new-made
  widows and orphans;
Strong men are full of glee because other strong men are
  either slain or doomed to rot alive in torments;
Small boys are delirious with pride and joy as they fancy
  themselves thrusting swords into soft flesh, and
  burning and laying waste such homes as they
  themselves inhabit;

Another capital is cast down with mourning and
    humiliation just in proportion as ours is raised up, and
    that is the very spice of our triumph . . .
This is life—this is patriotism—this is rapture!
But we—what are we, men or devils? and our Christian
    capital—what is it but an outpost of Hell?

*Ernest H. Crosby*


# Futility

Move him into the sun—
Gently its touch awoke him once,
At home, whispering of fields unsown.
Always it woke him, even in France,
Until this morning and this snow.
If anything might rouse him now
The kind old sun will know.

Think how it wakes the seeds,—
Woke, once, the clays of a cold star.
Are limbs, so dear-achieved, are sides,
Full-nerved—still warm—too hard to stir?
Was it for this the clay grew tall?
—O what made fatuous sunbeams toil
To break earth's sleep at all?

*Wilfred Owen*


When you see millions of the mouthless dead
Across your dreams in pale battalions go,
Say not soft things as other men have said,
That you'll remember. For you need not so.
Give them not praise. For, deaf, how should they know
It is not curses heaped on each gashed head?
Nor tears. Their blind eyes see not your tears flow.

Nor honour. It is easy to be dead.
Say only this, 'They are dead.' Then add thereto,
'Yet many a better one has died before.'
Then, scanning all the o'ercrowded mass, should you
Perceive one face that you loved heretofore,
It is a spook. None wears the face you knew.
Great death has made all his for evermore.

*Charles Sorley*


# Harp Song of the Dane Women

What is a woman that you forsake her,
And the hearth-fire and the home-acre,
To go with the old grey Widow-maker?

She has no house to lay a guest in—
But one chill bed for all to rest in,
That the pale suns and the stray bergs nest in:

She has no strong white arms to fold you,
But the ten-times-fingering weed to hold you—
Out on the rocks where the tide has rolled you.

Yet, when the signs of summer thicken,
And the ice breaks, and the birch-buds quicken,
Yearly you turn from our side, and sicken—

Sicken again for the shouts and the slaughters.
You steal away to the lapping waters,
And look at your ship in her winter-quarters.

You forget our mirth, and talk at the tables,
The kine in the shed and the horse in the stables—
To pitch her sides and go over her cables.

Then you drive out where the storm-clouds swallow,
And the sound of your oar-blades, falling hollow,
Is all we have left through the months to follow.

Ah, what is Woman that you forsake her,
And the hearth-fire and the home-acre,
To go with the old grey Widow-maker?

*Rudyard Kipling*

# Penelope

In the pathway of the sun,
    In the footsteps of the breeze,
Where the world and sky are one,
    He shall ride the silver seas,
        He shall cut the glittering wave.
I shall sit at home, and rock;
Rise, to heed a neighbour's knock;
Brew my tea, and snip my thread;
Bleach the linen for my bed.
        They will call him brave.

*Dorothy Parker*

# Glory of Women

You love us when we're heroes, home on leave,
Or wounded in a mentionable place.
You worship decorations; you believe
That chivalry redeems the war's disgrace.
You make us shells. You listen with delight,
By tales of dirt and danger fondly thrilled.
You crown our distant ardours while we fight,
And mourn our laurelled memories when we're killed.
You can't believe that British troops 'retire'
When hell's last horror breaks them, and they run,
Trampling the terrible corpses—blind with blood.
    O German mother dreaming by the fire,
    While you are knitting socks to send your son
    His face is trodden deeper in the mud.

*Siegfried Sassoon*

# War story

The story usually goes like this:
There were three men
And two of them were at home
Full of food
Cigarettes and beer
While the third
Was ignorant
Of the ways of the world
And wore a flag over his eyes.

The story sometimes goes like this:
There were three men
And two of them were yellow
The third was a Hero
Gorged with blood
And his mother and the patriots
Were proud of him.

Sometimes it goes like this:
There is a man
And he is running into battle
Wearing a flag over his eyes;
Three women wait
At home
For Word of their Hero
And his Famous Death:
These are his mother
His wife
And his sweetheart.
His mother is waiting
With her finger on the telephone
Ready to ring the undertaker.

*Roger Vincent Small*

# 1940

As I lay in the bath the air was filling with bells;
Over the steam of the window, out in the sun,
From the village below came hoarsely the patriot yells
And I knew that the next World War had at last begun.
As I lay in the bath I saw things clear in my head:
Ten to one they'd not bother to bomb us here,
Ten to one that they'd make for the barracks instead—
As I lay in the bath, I certainly saw things clear.
As I started to dry, came a humming of expectation;
Was it the enemy planes or was it young Jack
And the rest of the gang who have passed in their aviation
Setting across to Berlin to make an attack?
As the water gurgled away I put on a shirt,
I put on my trousers, and parted what's left of my hair,
And the humming above increased to a roaring spurt
And a shuddering thud drove all the bells from the air,
And a shuddering thud drove ev'rything else to silence.
There wasn't a sound, there wasn't a soul in the street,
There wasn't a wall to the house, there wasn't a staircase;
There was only the bathroom linoleum under my feet.
I called, as I always do, I called to Penelope,
I called to the strong with the petulant call of the weak;
There lay the head and the brown eyes dizzily open,
And the mouth apart but the tongue unable to speak;
There lay the nut-shaped head that I love for ever,
The thin little neck, the turned-up nose and the charms
Of pouting lips and lashes and circling eyebrows;
But where was the body? and where were the legs and
    arms?
And somewhere about I must seek in the broken building,
Somewhere about they'll probably find my son.
Oh bountiful Gods of the air! Oh Science and Progress!
You great big wonderful world! Oh what have you done?

*John Betjeman*

I climb that wooded hill
And look towards where my father is.
My father is saying, 'Alas, my son is on service;
Day and night he knows no rest.
Grant that he is being careful of himself,
So that he may come back and not be left behind!'

I climb that bare hill
And look towards where my mother is.
My mother is saying, 'Alas, my young one is on service;
Day and night he gets no sleep.
Grant that he is being careful of himself,
So that he may come back, and not be cast away.'

I climb that ridge
And look towards where my elder brother is.
My brother is saying, 'Alas, my young brother is on service;
Day and night he toils.
Grant that he is being careful of himself,
So that he may come back and not die.'

*from Book of Songs*
*translated from the Chinese by Arthur Waley*

# 15th March 1939

And she said
*The Germans have marched into Prague.*
And she said
THE GER-MANS HAVE MARCHED IN-TO PRAGUE.
Careless, eleven,
I smile comprehension.
(Or was it embarrassment?
Or was it a not-wanting-to-know?
How can I tell now
so many years later?)
And I wrote in my letter
*What are*
*the German uniforms like?*
And my father replying,
(and my father forgiving me):
*Not bad*
*as uniforms go.*

*Gerda Mayer*

# Post-war

In 1943
my father
dropped bombs on the continent

I remember
my mother
talking about bananas
in 1944

when it rained,
creeping alone to the windowsill,
I stared up the hill,
watching, watching,
watching without a blink
for the Mighty Bananas
to stride through the blitz

they came in paper bags
in neighbours' hands
when they came
and took their time
over the coming

and still I don't know
where my father
flying home
took a wrong turning

*Libby Houston*

# I Saw a Film one Sunday

I saw a film one Sunday
Called 'Oh! What a Lovely War.'
I couldn't understand it—
But what were they fighting for?

Great Grandad says he was 'in it'—
Fighting the war, I mean.
But he doesn't know what he fought for,
And he just wouldn't say what he'd seen.

*John Kitching*

# Easter Monday

*(In Memoriam E.T.)*

In the last letter that I had from France
You thanked me for the silver Easter egg
Which I had hidden in the box of apples
You liked to munch beyond all other fruit.
You found the egg the Monday before Easter,
And said, 'I will praise Easter Monday now—
It was such a lovely morning'. Then you spoke
Of the coming battle and said, 'This is the eve.
Good-bye. And may I have a letter soon.'

That Easter Monday was a day for praise,
It was such a lovely morning. In our garden
We sowed our earliest seeds, and in the orchard
The apple-bud was ripe. It was the eve.
There are three letters that you will not get.

*Eleanor Farjeon*
*April 9th, 1917*

# The Medal

When the telegram arrived
I was combing my hair in the sun
And gossiping with the servants.
It said the Government were sorry
My husband was dead, killed in action.
For two days I did not know
What had happened. Then I woke
To mother's voice in the next room
Comforting a weeping neighbour
(As if she were the bereaved one).
Slowly, full consciousness returned.
I dressed for the first time as a widow.
I ate my first meal as a widow.
When I was resigned to thinking of him
As lying scattered in a rice-field,
A thighbone here, a breastbone there,
The rest gifted to the vultures,
They printed his name in the papers
And a photograph of his bachelor days.
He had died a hero.
The friends trooped in again
This time to congratulate.
I heard my father accepting
The tributes with a tired mouth.
I was invited to the ceremony
Where the general gave me a medal
And patted my son on the head.
For an entire week the little fellow
Strutted around the bazaar
With the medal pinned on his shirt,
And the neighbours gave him sweets.

Now the medal is lying in its box
And is taken out less and less.
What shall I do with it?
A medal has no hands, no lips, no genitals
It is exactly what it looks like:
Just another piece of bronze.

*Taufiq Rafat*

# Hieronymus Bosch, we can do it

Now we can burn a gesture into stone.
The sky will wink and drop birds,
winds shuffle skin like paper in a gutter.
We can reduce all difference to one.

And we can astonish with such a sun
cities will spring right open; concrete
blossom and seed; dust celebrate total summer
and ultimate winter in one.

These modern miracles are too clever
for the fools who made all those fables:
gently Persephone would waken earth.
They were to last for ever.

*Paul Coltman*




# Ghosts, Fire, Water

*On the Hiroshima panels by Iri Maruki and Toshiko
    Akamatsu*

These are the ghosts of the unwilling dead,
Grey ghosts of that imprinted flash of memory
Whose flaming and eternal instant haunts
The speechless dark with dread and anger.

Grey, out of pale nothingness their agony appears.
Like ash they are blown and blasted on the wind's
Vermilion breathlessness, like shapeless smoke
Their shapes are torn across the paper sky.

These scarred and ashen ghosts are quick
With pain's unutterable speech, their flame-cracked flesh
Writhes and is heavy as the worms, the bitter dirt;
Lonely as in death they bleed, naked as in birth.

They greet each other in a ghastly paradise,
These ghosts who cannot come with gifts and flowers.
Here they receive each other with disaster's common love,
Covering one another's pain with shrivelled hands.

They are not beautiful, yet beauty is in their truth.
There is no easy music in their silent screams,
No ordered dancing in their grief's distracted limbs.
Their shame is ours. We, too, are haunted by their fate.

In the shock of flame, their tears brand our flesh,
We twist in their furnace, and our scorching throats
Parch for the waters where the cool dead float.
We press our lips upon the river where they drink, and
          drown.

Their voices call to us, in pain and indignation:
'This is what you have done to us!'
—Their accusation is our final hope. Be comforted.
Yes, we have heard you, ghosts of our indifference,

We hear your cry, we understand your warnings.
We, too, shall refuse to accept our fate!
Haunt us with the truth of our betrayal
Until the earth's united voices shout refusal, sing your
          peace!

Forgive us, that we had to see your passion to remember
What we must never again deny: *Love one another.*

*James Kirkup*

# The Kimono

Celebrate the season of the death of the city.
Celebrate the woman in the newsreel, the print of her ki-
  mono
Burned in her back. Celebrate the bamboo leaves, the
      folded fans.

Exhibit A, formerly a person, was born as the white plant
    bloomed;
She is the night dream of the spectator, incised on the lid-
    less eye;
Woman without face or name that is known lives in my
    house.

Weigh her, measure her, peer for children
in her clouded history; check with Geiger counters
the click of the doomed leaves and fans.

Lost in events the beauty and the grace of women;
Ended the age of natural love as the bomb bay opened
On the burned shoulders: she is now the memorable one.

From the nightmare to the eye
from the eye to the house
from the house to the heart
enter the dimension of love:

woman of Hiroshima
be merciful to the merciless!

*Don Gordon*

# Monuments of Hiroshima

The roughly estimated ones, who do not sort well
   with our common phrases,
Who are by no means eating roots of dandelion,
   or pushing up the daisies.

The more or less anonymous, to whom no human idiom
   can apply,
Who neither passed away, or on,
   nor went before, nor vanished on a sigh.

Little of peace for them to rest in, less of them
   to rest in peace:
Dust to dust a swift transition, ashes to ash
   with awful ease.

Their only monument will be of others' casting—
A Tower of Peace, a Hall of Peace, a Bridge of Peace
   —who might have wished for something lasting,
Like a wooden box.

*D. J. Enright*

# They Dared Him

Tommy has dropped his Atom Bomb
Upon the nursery floor
Until the dust has cleared away
His little brothers cannot play
Toy soldiers any more.

Teddy's hair is falling out
From Gamma radiation
Jane will have a busy hols,
Six defenceless little dolls
Need decontamination.

You should have seen the mushroom cloud
Rise upwards to the ceiling.
Nanny says they can avoid
Having all the cows destroyed
As some of them are healing.

Tommy has dropped his Atom Bomb
Upon the nursery floor.
He has completely spoilt the fun,
It takes an ordinary gun
To make a decent war.

*Kevin Myhill*

# Crusader

in bed
like a dead
crusader

arms folded a
cross my chest
i lie

eyes closed
listening
to the bodys glib mechanics
\* \* \*

on the street
outside
men of violence

quarrel
their drunken voices
dark weals

on the
glistening
back of the night

*Roger McGough*

# Remember They Say

Remember they say the dead
who will rise again
Remember in November
littered bones and ashes of men
in Flanders, Dunkirk, Korea
Burma, Hiroshima
murdered in cold calculation

Remember the scarlet heads
on execution mornings
candid Bavarian mornings

green heaps of human marble
children dying to prove innocence.
Remember the aching
silence of despair,
the strangled silence of the moon
in men's hearts

Remember, yes remember
with trumpets and guns
the helping hand
dripping with blood
Remember the menace is still with us

Remember also the living
two billion weary souls
Let them also have trumpets
for the future has a stronger memory
than the past.

*Lenrie Peters*

# Concord Hymn

Sung at the completion of the Battle Monument, 19 April 1836

By the rude bridge that arched the flood,
   Their flag to April's breeze unfurled,
Here once the embattled farmers stood,
   And fired the shot heard round the world.

The foe long since in silence slept;
   Alike the conqueror silent sleeps;
And Time the ruined bridge has swept
   Down the dark stream which seaward creeps.

On this green bank, by this soft stream,
   We set today a votive stone;
That memory may their deed redeem,
   When, like our sires, our sons are gone.

Spirit, that made those heroes dare
   To die, and leave their children free,
Bid Time and Nature gently spare
   The shaft we raise to them and thee.

*Ralph Waldo Emerson*

# The Tomb of Lieutenant John Learmonth, A.I.F.

At the end of Crete he took to the hills, and said he'd fight it out with a revolver. He was a great soldier.
*—One of his men in a letter*

This is not sorrow, this is work: I build
A cairn of words over a silent man,
My friend John Learmonth whom the Germans killed.

There was no word of hero in his plan;
Verse should have been his love and peace his trade,
But history turned him to a partisan.

For from the battle as his bones are laid
Crete will remember him. Remember well,
Mountains of Crete, the Second Field Brigade!

Say Crete, and there is little more to tell
Of muddle tall as treachery, despair
And black defeat resounding like a bell;

But bring the magnifying focus near
And in contempt of muddle and defeat
The old heroic virtues still appear.

Australian blood where hot and icy meet
(James Hogg and Lermontov were of his kin)
Lie still and fertilize the fields of Crete.

*             *             *

Schoolboy, I watched his ballading begin:
Billy and bullocky and billabong,
Our properties of childhood, all were in.

I hear the air though not the undersong,
The fierceness and resolve; but all the same
They're the tradition, and tradition's strong.

Swagman and bushranger die hard, die game,
Die fighting, like that wild colonial boy—
Jack Dowling, says the ballad, was his name.

He also spun his pistol like a toy,
Turned to the hills like a wolf or kangaroo,
And faced destruction with a bitter joy.

His freedom gave him nothing else to do
But set his back against his family tree
And fight the better for the fact he knew

He was as good as dead. Because the sea
Was closed and the air dark and the land lost,
'They'll never capture me alive,' said he.

                    *         *         *

That's courage chemically pure, uncrossed
With sacrifice or duty or career,
Which counts and pays in ready coin the cost

Of holding course. Armies are not its sphere
Where all's contrived to achieve its counterfeit;
It swears with discipline, its volunteer.

I could as hardly make a moral fit
Around it as around a lightning flash.
There is no moral, that's the point of it,

No moral, but I'm glad of this panache
That sparkles, as from flint, from us and steel,
True to no crown nor presidential sash

Nor flag nor fame. Let others mourn and feel
He died for nothing: nothings have their place.
While thus the kind and civilized conceal

This spring of unsuspected inward grace
And look on death as equals, I am filled
With queer affection for the human race.

*J. S. Manifold*

# Beach Burial

Softly and humbly to the Gulf of Arabs
The convoys of dead sailors come;
At night they sway and wander in the waters far under,
But morning rolls them in the foam.

Between the sob and clubbing of the gunfire
Someone, it seems, has time for this,
To pluck them from the shallows and bury them in burrows
And tread the sand upon their nakedness;

And each cross, the driven stake of tidewood,
Bears the last signature of men,
Written with such perplexity, with such bewildered pity,
The words choke as they begin—

'Unknown seaman'—the ghostly pencil
Wavers and fades, the purple drips,
The breath of the wet season has washed their inscriptions
As blue as drowned men's lips,

Dead seamen, gone in search of the same landfall,
Whether as enemies they fought,
Or fought with us, or neither; the sand joins them together,
Enlisted on the other front.

*El Alamein*
*Kenneth Slessor*

It feels a shame to be Alive—
When Men so brave—are dead—
One envies the Distinguished Dust—
Permitted—such a Head—

The Stone—that tells defending Whom
This Spartan put away
What little of Him we—possessed
In Pawn for Liberty—

The price is great—Sublimely paid—
Do we deserve—a Thing—
That lives—like Dollars—must be piled
Before we may obtain?

Are we that wait—sufficient worth—
That such Enormous Pearl
As life—dissolved be—for Us—
In Battle's—horrid Bowl?

It may be—a Renown to live—
I think the Men who die—
Those unsustained—Saviours—
Present Divinity—

*Emily Dickinson*

## At the British War Cemetery, Bayeux

I walked where in their talking graves
And shirts of earth five thousand lay,
When history with ten feasts of fire
Had eaten the red air away.

I am Christ's boy, I cried, I bear
In iron hands the bread, the fishes.
I hang with honey and with rose
This tidy wreck of all your wishes.

On your geometry of sleep
The chestnut and the fir-tree fly,
And lavender and marguerite
Forge with their flowers an English sky.

Turn now towards the belling town
Your jigsaws of impossible bone,
And rising read your rank of snow
Accurate as death upon the stone.

About your easy heads my prayers
I said with syllables of clay.
What gift, I asked, shall I bring now
Before I weep and walk away?

Take, they replied, the oak and laurel,
Take our fortune of tears and live
Like a spendthrift lover. All we ask
Is the one gift you cannot give.

*Charles Causley*

# Lunchtime Lecture

And this from the second or third millenium
B.C., a female, aged about twenty-two.
A white, fine skull, full up with darkness
As a shell with sea, drowned in the centuries.
Small, perfect. The cranium would fit the palm
Of a man's hand. Some plague or violence
Destroyed her, and her whiteness lay safe in a shroud
Of silence, undisturbed, unrained on, dark
For four thousand years. Till a tractor in summer
Biting its way through the longcairn for supplies
Of stone, broke open the grave and let a crowd of light
Stare in at her, and she stared quietly back.

As I look at her I feel none of the shock
The farmer felt as, unprepared, he found her.
Here in the Museum, like death in hospital,
Reasons are given, labels, causes, catalogues.
The smell of death is done. Left, only her bone
Purity, the light and shade beauty that her man
Was denied sight of, the perfect edge of the place
Where the pieces join, with no mistakes, like boundaries.

She's a tree in winter, stripped white on a black sky,
Leafless formality, brow, bough in fine relief.
I, at some other season, illustrate the tree
Fleshed, with woman's hair and colours and the rustling
Blood, the troubled mind that she has overthrown.
We stare at each other, dark into sightless
Dark, seeing only ourselves in the black pools,
Gulping the risen sea that booms in the shell.

*Gillian Clarke*

# Cissbury Ring

The plain is alive with shadow: rout of rags
and tattered banners hurrying away. Deserted now
save for a solitary horseman
far off, sauntering along a dusty track.
The walls I lean on winds have rounded;
murmuring summers levelled the ditch, moulded
toothed scarp to the hill's shoulder.
Two thousand years: time's slow explosion still
scattering daggers and axeheads and dust of bones.
Quiet sounds: a drowsy burden of grasshoppers;
the wind's thin bugle bending ranks of grass.
No shouting at the gate now. Warriors silent,
their long bronze trumpets choked with earth.

*Paul Coltman*




# Tolquhon Castle

Old, the curator wields his heavy
key, and takes your toll.
(*He* is the laird now.)

Green-carpeted his gatehouse, suave and varnished,
history-hung. There loom
the blinded granite walls.

His peasant grandson, motor-mad,
proprietory, boasts
how he cuts lawns . . .

where once a courtyard stank of beast and man.
My Lady's chamber bare;
and scoured by storm, the gallery.

A North-Sea wind that might have sneaked past wrought
hinge and murky glass
to stir the hanging plaid

shoots through the gunports, sweeping
buttery and brewhouse; whirls
up the domestic stair

littered with dung, pellets of bone and fur.
There, dynastic owls
flap in from moonlit hills,

shriek out each night their noble tenure, glide
out, rapacious ghosts,
while the man dreams

of dead loves, old wars;
and the boy . . .
of engines.

*Margaret Toms*


# Return to Sedgemoor

'Battle of Sedgemoor. Come and bring your friends.'
And so they have I see. Dragging me down
Into this pageant of what was once real.
I died here but I cannot now recall
Which side I fought on. And until today—
Comfortable in warm weather hoping something,
Tetchy in winter dreading everything—
I've been content simply to know I was
Once here. How shocking the oblivion
Of coming back to sight and sound, to north
And south, to right and wrong, at a complete loss.

The cows are gazing at the popping cannon.
What roars they must have heard to go on chewing
At noise that shot the meat out of our mouths.
I seem to see the guns for the first time,
Plump little pigs. I hear a voice explaining
That they were known as 'Hot Lips' and 'Sweet Lips'.
I swear we never called them anything
Like that. I first made love on a battlefield,
I remember—though not which or who—
And realized there was a difference
Between love and war: I don't remember what.

Sedgemoor took place at night, and it's enough
To make a ghost laugh in the sun to see
These fluent creatures dash about regardless
While we, with elbows, knees and arse and chin
Stuck out at angles, had to feel our way.
These willow trees were low and strong to hang
Men in the morning light—as they are doing
Now—but in the dark they merely gave
Us bloody noses. Memory does not return
Like experience, more like imagination:
How it would have been if, how it must.

'The last battle to be fought on English soil'
The voice concludes. No riots, no pretenders
Or invaders in what must be years?
No, I am a ghost and do not wish
To understand the present. Let me
Concentrate on getting my life back.
My memory is like a severed muscle
And there's no friend or foe or animal
To recognize me. On the night I died
King's men and rebels all hastened away
As if some moon came up to light them home.

*Patricia Beer*

# In Flanders Fields

In Flanders fields the poppies blow
Between the crosses, row on row,
    That mark our place; and in the sky
    The larks, still bravely singing, fly
Scarce heard amid the guns below.

We are the Dead. Short days ago
We lived, felt dawn, saw sunset glow,
    Loved and were loved, and now we lie
        In Flanders fields.

Take up our quarrel with the foe:
To you from failing hands we throw
    The torch; be yours to hold it high.
    If ye break faith with us who die
We shall not sleep, though poppies grow
        In Flanders fields.

*John McCrae*


# High Wood

Ladies and gentlemen, this is High Wood,
Called by the French, Bois des Fourneaux;
The famous spot which in Nineteen-Sixteen
July, August and September was the scene
Of long and bitterly contested strife,
By reason of its High commanding site.
Observe the effect of shell-fire in the trees
Standing and fallen; here is wire; this trench
For months inhabited, twelve times changed hands;
(They soon fall in), used later as a grave.
It has been said on good authority
That in the fighting for this patch of wood

Were killed somewhere above eight thousand men,
Of whom the greater part were buried here,
This mound on which you stand being . . .
                                    Madame, please,
You are requested kindly not to touch
Or take away the Company's property
As souvenirs; you'll find we have on sale
A large variety, all guaranteed.
As I was saying, all is as it was,
This is an unknown British officer,
The tunic having lately rotted off.
Please follow me—this way . . .
                          the *path*, sir, *please*,
The ground which was secured at great expense
The Company keeps absolutely untouched,
And in that dug-out (genuine) we provide
Refreshments at a reasonable rate.
You are requested not to leave about
Paper, or ginger-beer bottles, or orange-peel,
There are waste-paper baskets at the gate.

*Philip Johnstone*

# Magpies in Picardy

The magpies in Picardy
Are more than I can tell.
They flicker down the dusty roads
And cast a magic spell
On the men who march through Picardy,
Through Picardy to Hell.

(The blackbird flies with panic,
The swallow goes like light,
The finches move like ladies,
The owl floats by at night;
But the great and flashing magpie
He flies as artists might.)

A magpie in Picardy
Told me secret things—
Of the music in white feathers,
And the sunlight that sings
And dances in deep shadows—
He told me with his wings.

(The hawk is cruel and rigid,
He watches from a height;
The rook is slow and sombre,
The robin loves to fight;
But the great and flashing magpie
He flies as lovers might.)

He told me that in Picardy,
An age ago or more,
While all his fathers still were eggs,
These dusty highways bore
Brown singing soldiers marching out
Through Picardy to war.

He said that still through chaos
Works on the ancient plan
And two things have altered not
Since first the world began—
The beauty of the wild green earth
And the bravery of man.

(For the sparrow flies unthinking
And quarrels in his flight;
The heron trails his legs behind,
The lark goes out of sight;
But the great and flashing magpie
He flies as poets might.)

*T. P. Cameron Wilson*


# Beaucourt Revisited

I wandered up to Beaucourt, I took the river track,
And saw the lines we lived in before the Boche went back;
But Peace was now in Pottage, the front was far ahead,
The front had journeyed Eastward, and only left the dead.

And I thought, How long we lay there, and watched across the wire,
While the guns roared round the valley, and set the skies afire!
But now there are homes in Hamel and tents in the Vale of Hell,
And a Camp at Suicide Corner, where half a regiment fell.

The new troops follow after, and tread the land we won,
To them 'tis so much hillside re-wrested from the Hun;
We only walk with reverence this sullen mile of mud;
The shell-holes hold our history, and half of them our
    blood.

Here, at the head of Peche Street, 'twas death to show your face;
To me it seemed like magic to linger in the place;
For me how many spirits hung round the Kentish Caves,
But the new men see no spirits—they only see the graves.

I found the half-dug ditches we fashioned for the fight.
We lost a score of men there—young James was killed that night;
I saw the star-shells staring, I heard the bullets hail,
But the new troops pass unheeding—they never heard the tale.

I crossed the blood-red ribbon, that once was No Man's Land,
I saw a misty daybreak and a creeping minute-hand;
And here the lads went over, and there was Harmsworth shot,
And here was William lying—but the new men know them not.

And I said, 'There is still the river, and still the stiff, stark trees:
To treasure here our story, but there are only these;'
But under the white wood crosses the dead men answered
        low,
'The new men know not Beaucourt, but we are here—we know.'

*A. P. Herbert*

# An Airstrip in Essex, 1960

It is a lost road into the air.
It is a desert
among sugar beets.
The tiny wings
of the Spitfires of nineteen-forty-one
flake in the mud of the Channel.

Near the road a brick pillbox
totters under a load of grass,
where Home Guards waited
in the white fogs of the invasion winter.

Goodnight, old ruined war.

In Poland the wind rides on a jagged wall.
Smoke rises from the stones; no, it is mist.

*Donald Hall*

# Now We Are Six

My daddy's dressing up as Father Christmas
  With presents for the stocking and the tree—
I know he is, because he's always Santa Claus,
  And it used to take me in, when I was three.
I did believe in fairies, and in Santa,
  But definitely stopped when I was four;
It isn't that I won't, but simply that I don't
    Any more.

When mummies shop to make a merry Christmas
  It's up to kiddies all to play the game—
I wouldn't be the one to spoil the parents' fun,
  And my little baby sister says the same.
The parents think we still believe in fairies,
  But we have heard and seen an awful lot.
They think that games and holly and things will make us
    jolly—
    Well, we're not.

It's clear to me the whole world situation
  Has gone from bad to worse since I was five—
We kiddies are agreed, from all we hear and read,
  Next Christmas we mayn't even be alive.
I've talked it over with my baby sister,
  It sometimes makes us feel a little blue—
We want to go to heaven, but not before we're seven,
    Well, would you?

When I was one, a bomb came down the chimney,
  When I was two, they said war clouds had passed—
Now veterans in the nursery this Christmas anniversary
  Expect it may be probably their last.
With all the nations of the earth rearming
  We feel it's the beginning of the end.
We're really not neurotic, but I think it idiotic
    To pretend.

When Daddy's dressing up as Father Christmas,
    When grown-ups are enjoying Christmas fun,
It makes the children glad to think that mum and dad
    Have not the least idea what's going on.
We want to be good democratic kiddies,
    My baby sister loves the common cause—
But sometimes she and I confess we wonder why
    Grown-ups can still believe in Santa Claus.

*Sagittarius*


# Your Attention Please

The Polar DEW has just warned that
A nuclear rocket strike of
At least one thousand megatons
Has been launched by the enemy
Directly at our major cities.
This announcement will take
Two and a quarter minutes to make,
You therefore have a further
Eight and a quarter minutes
To comply with the shelter
Requirements published in the Civil
Defence Code—section Atomic Attack.
A specially shortened Mass
Will be broadcast at the end
Of this announcement—
Protestant and Jewish services
Will begin simultaneously—
Select your wavelength immediately
According to instructions
In the Defence Code. Do not
Take well-loved pets (including birds)
Into your shelter—they will consume
Fresh air. Leave the old and bed-
ridden, you can do nothing for them.
Remember to press the sealing

Switch when everyone is in
The shelter. Set the radiation
Aerial, turn on the geiger barometer.
Turn off your Television now.
Turn off your radio immediately
The Services end. At the same time
Secure explosion plugs in the ears
Of each member of your family. Take
Down your plasma flasks. Give your children
The pills marked one and two
In the C.D. green container, then put
Them to bed. Do not break
The inside airlock seals until
The radiation All Clear shows
(Watch for the cuckoo in your
perspex panel), or your District
Touring Doctor rings your bell.
If before this, your air becomes
Exhausted or if any of your family
Is critically injured, administer
The capsules marked 'Valley Forge'
(Red pocket in No. 1 Survival Kit)
For painless death. (Catholics
Will have been instructed by their priests
What to do in this eventuality.)
This announcement is ending. Our President
Has already given order for
Massive retaliation—it will be
Decisive. Some of us may die.
Remember, statistically
It is not likely to be you.
All flags are flying fully dressed
On Government buildings—the sun is shining.
Death is the least we have to fear.
We are all in the hands of God,
Whatever happens happens by His Will.
Now go quickly to your shelters.

*Peter Porter*

# A History Lesson

Kings
like golden gleams
made with a mirror on the wall.

A non-alcoholic pope,
knights without arms,
arms without knights.

The dead like so many stained noodles,
a pound of those fallen in battle,
two ounces of those who were executed,

several heads
like so many potatoes
shaken into a cap—

Geniuses conceived
by the mating of dates
are soaked up by the ceiling into infinity

to the sound of tinny thunder,
the rumble of bellies,
shouts of hurrah,

empires rise and fall
at a wave of the pointer,
the blood is blotted out—

And only one small boy,
who was not paying the least attention,
will ask
between two victorious wars:

And did it hurt in those days too?

*Miroslav Holub*
*translated from the Czech by George Theiner*

# Prayer Before Birth

I am not yet born; O hear me.
Let not the bloodsucking bat or the rat or the stoat or the club-
    footed ghoul come near me.

I am not yet born, console me.
I fear that the human race may with tall walls wall me,
    with strong drugs dope me, with wise lies lure me,
        on black racks rack me, in blood-baths roll me.

I am not yet born; provide me
With water to dandle me, grass to grow for me, trees to talk to
    me, sky to sing to me, birds and a white light
        in the back of my mind to guide me.

I am not yet born; forgive me
For the sins that in me the world shall commit, my words
    my treason engendered by traitors beyond me,
        my life when they murder by means of my
            hands, my death when they live me.

I am not yet born; rehearse me
In the parts I must play and the cues I must take when
    old men lecture me, bureaucrats hector me, mountains
        frown at me, lovers laugh at me, the white
            waves call me to folly and the desert calls
                me down to doom and the beggar refuses
                    my gift and my children curse me.

I am not yet born; O hear me,
Let not the man who is beast or who thinks he is God
    come near me.

I am not yet born; O fill me
With strength against those who would freeze my
    humanity, would dragoon me into a lethal automaton,
        would make me a cog in a machine, a thing with
            one face, a thing, and against all those
                who would dissipate my entirety, would
                    blow me like thistledown hither and
                        thither or hither and thither like
                            water held in the
                                hands would spill me.
Let them not make me a stone and let them not spill me.
Otherwise kill me.

*Louis MacNeice*


# Conscientious Objector

I shall die, but that is all that I shall do for Death.

I hear him leading his horse out of the stall; I hear the
    clatter on the barn-floor.
He is in haste; he has business in Cuba, business in the
    Balkans, many calls to make this morning.
But I will not hold the bridle while he cinches the
    girth.
And he may mount by himself; I will not give him a
    leg up.

Though he flick my shoulders with his whip, I will not
    tell him which way the fox ran.
With his hoof on my breast, I will not tell him where
    the black boy hides in the swamp.
I shall die, but that is all that I shall do for Death; I
    am not on his pay-roll.

I will not tell him the whereabouts of my friends nor
    of my enemies either.
Though he promise me much, I will not map him the
    route to any man's door.

Am I a spy in the land of the living, that I should
 deliver men to Death?
Brother, the password and the plans of our city are
 safe with me; never through me
Shall you be overcome.

*Edna St. Vincent Millay*


# The Horses

Barely a twelvemonth after
The seven days war that put the world to sleep,
Late in the evening the strange horses came
By then we had made our covenant with silence,
But in the first few days it was so still
We listened to our breathing and were afraid.
On the second day
The radios failed; we turned the knobs; no answer.
On the third day a warship passed us, heading north,
Dead bodies piled on the deck. On the sixth day
A plane plunged over us into the sea. Thereafter
Nothing. The radios dumb;
And still they stand in corners of our kitchens,
And stand, perhaps, turned on, in a million rooms
All over the world. But now if they should speak,
If on a sudden they should speak again,
If on the stroke of noon a voice should speak,
We would not listen, we would not let it bring
That old bad world that swallowed its children quick
At one great gulp. We would not have it again.
Sometimes we think of the nations lying asleep,
Curled blindly in impenetrable sorrow,
And then the thought confounds us with its strangeness.
The tractors lie about our fields; at evening
They look like dank sea-monsters couched and waiting.
We leave them where they are and let them rust:

'They'll moulder away and be like other loam.'
We make our oxen drag our rusty ploughs,
Long laid aside. We have gone back
Far past our fathers' land.
                              And then, that evening
Late in the summer the strange horses came.
We heard a distant tapping on the road,
A deepening drumming; it stopped, went on again
And at the corner changed to hollow thunder.
We saw the heads
Like a wild wave charging and were afraid.
We had sold our horses in our fathers' time
To buy new tractors. Now they were strange to us
As fabulous steeds set on an ancient shield
Or illustrations in a book of knights.
We did not dare go near them. Yet they waited,
Stubborn and shy, as if they had been sent
By an old command to find our whereabouts
And that long-lost archaic companionship.
In the first moment we had never a thought
That they were creatures to be owned and used.
Among them were some half-a-dozen colts
Dropped in some wilderness of the broken world,
Yet new as if they had come from their own Eden.
Since then they have pulled our ploughs and borne our
loads
But that free servitude still can pierce our hearts.
Our life is changed; their coming our beginning.

*Edwin Muir*

# The Second Coming

Turning and turning in the widening gyre
The falcon cannot hear the falconer;
Things fall apart; the centre cannot hold;
Mere anarchy is loosed upon the world,
The blood-dimmed tide is loosed and everywhere
The ceremony of innocence is drowned;
The best lack all conviction, while the worst
Are full of passionate intensity.

Surely some revelation is at hand;
Surely the Second Coming is at hand.
The Second Coming! Hardly are those words out
When a vast image out of Spiritus Mundi
Troubles my sight: somewhere in sands of the desert
A shape with lion body and the head of a man,
A gaze blank and pitiless as the sun,
Is moving its slow thighs, while all about it
Reel shadows of the indignant desert birds.
The darkness drops again; but now I know
That twenty centuries of stony sleep
Were vexed to nightmare by a rocking cradle,
And what rough beast, its hour come round at last,
Slouches towards Bethlehem to be born?

*W. B. Yeats*

# The Four Horsemen

And I saw when the Lamb opened one of the seals,
and I heard, as it were the noise of thunder,
one of the four beasts saying, Come and see.
And I saw, and behold a white horse:
and he that sat on him had a bow;
and a crown was given unto him:
and he went forth conquering, and to conquer.

And when he had opened the second seal,
I heard the second beast say, Come and see.
And there went out another horse that was red:
and power was given to him that sat thereon
to take peace from the earth,
and that they should kill one another:
and there was given unto him a great sword.

And when he had opened the third seal,
I heard the third beast say, Come and see.
And I beheld, and lo a black horse;
and he that sat on him had a pair of balances in his hand.
And I heard a voice in the midst of the four beasts say,
A measure of wheat for a penny,
and three measures of barley for a penny,
and see thou hurt not the oil and the wine.

And when he had opened the fourth seal,
I heard the voice of the fourth beast say, Come and see.
And I looked and behold a pale horse:
and his name that sat on him was Death,
and Hell followed with him.
And power was given unto them over the fourth part of the earth,
to kill with sword,
and with hunger,
and with death,
and with the beasts of the earth.

*Revelation 6: 1–8*
*The Bible: King James Version*

# The Human Tyrants

Thomas hit and hit
Killing thousands of what
He thought to be warships
And the enemy.

Mary hit them unawares
As they ran from their hole
In the rotten tree-trunk
She thought—'A good job well done.'

I watched, spellbound with
Horror, real horror
And I thought bitterly—
Tiny lives, meaninglessly destroyed.

Think of being an ant
Killed for no reason.
They've done no wrong—
We're human tyrants.

*Alison Murdoch*

## Small Aircraft

As if I didn't have enough
Bothering me, now I'm confused
By dreaming nightly
Of small airplanes. I don't understand it.

The planes don't care that I dream of them:
Now like chickens they peck seed
From my hand. Now like termites
They live in the walls of my house.

Or else they poke me
With their dumb noses: little fish
Move like this to a child's foot,
Tickling, making their feet laugh.

Sometimes they push and bump each other
Around my fire, blinded by the light.
They won't let me read and the noise
Of their wings excites me.

They have another trick: they come
To me like children in tears
And sit in my lap,
Crying, *Take us in your arms.*

You can drive them away, but they're right back,
Flying out of the polished darkness,
Looking from their eyes like sad dachshunds
As their long bodies float by.

*Bella Akhmadulina*

179

# Between Battles

The roar of cannon
Has died away,
The reports of rifles
have become sporadic,
A few weary bugle calls
Can be faintly heard in the distance,
But they are neither for the retreat,
Nor for the charge.

The smoke of gunpowder
Is dispersing with the wind,
The battlefield
Is covered in silence;
Medical orderlies
Are busy dressing the wounded,
Stretcher teams
Are busy rushing here and there.

'Hu—lu, hu—lu. . . .'
Those who are too sleepy
Are snoring soundly
In sweet dreams.
'So you're still alive!'
The mischievous youths
Are joking
To amuse themselves.

On the battleground,
Things do not always
Remain at the same tempo.
Now there are
No gunfire and flames;
Above in the sky,
Pairs of colourful butterflies
Are fluttering around rifle muzzles;
Below in the field
Horses are gently
Nibbling at patches of turf. . . .

*Zhang Zhimin*

# The Ridge : 1919

Here on the ridge where the shrill north-easter trails
Low clouds along the snow,
And in a streaming moonlit vapour veils
The peopled earth below,

Let me, O life, a little while forget
The horror of past years—
Man and his agony and bloody sweat,
The terror and the tears,

And struggle only with the mist and snow
Against the hateless wind,
Till scourged and shriven I again may go
To dwell among my kind.

*Wilfrid Gibson*


# Shiloh
## A requiem
## (April, 1862)

Skimming lightly, wheeling still,
   The swallows fly low
Over the field in clouded days,
   The forest-field of Shiloh—.
Over the field where April rain
Solaced the parched ones stretched in pain
Through the pause of night
That followed the Sunday fight
   Around the church of Shiloh—
The church so lone, the long-built one,
That echoed to many a parting groan
     And natural prayer
  Of dying foemen mingled there—

Foeman at morn, but friends at eve—
    Fame or country least their care:
(What like a bullet can undeceive!)
    But now they lie low,
While over them the swallows skim,
    And all is hushed at Shiloh.

*Herman Melville*

# Everyone Sang

Everyone suddenly burst out singing;
And I was filled with such delight
As prisoned birds must find in freedom,
Winging wildly across the white
Orchards and dark-green fields; on—on—and out of sight.

Everyone's voice was suddenly lifted;
And beauty came like the setting sun:
My heart was shaken with tears; and horror
Drifted away . . . O, but Everyone
Was a bird; and the song was wordless; the singing will never be done.

*Siegfried Sassoon*

# Peace

Sing again the great song,
Sing it with the winds that are shaking the reeds.
Sing until the whole earth is shaken by the song.
Maybe summer may yet come again.

They summon you, who stand at the ruins.
They praise your once great kingdom,
Teeming with free men.
Across, in the villages devastated by war, they are calling
Saying: 'Come you who broke the battle axe,
Men are cutting men on the river bed.'
The waters that ran with the rainbow
Are curled with clots of blood;
The new seedlings sprout no more.
But you who speak with a dream
You will visit us
And unveil the new age
Letting us sleep on our backs
Listening to the multitudes of the stars.

*Mazisi Kunene*


# Armistice

It is finished. The enormous dust-cloud over Europe
Lifts like a million swallows; and a light
Drifting in craters, touches the quiet dead.

Now, at the bugle's hour, before the blood
Cakes in a clean wind on their marble faces,
Making them monuments; before the sun,

Hung like a medal on the smoky noon,
Whitens the bone that feeds the earth, before
Wheat-ear springs green, again, in the green spring

And they are bread in the bodies of the young:
Be strong to remember how the bread died, screaming;
Gangrene was corn, and monuments went mad.

*Paul Dehn*

# Landscape With Tanks

The tanks speed through the still, grey afternoon.
In drab villages straddling the road
shabby people cluster bewilderedly,
wave listlessly at the unmindful convoy.
If they raise a thin cheer, it goes unheard by the soldiers,
armour-cocooned, insulated by engine-roar, track-clatte1
and their own thoughts from this winter landscape
and its sombre figures.

'Never knew about them before, did you, Corp?'
Trooper Boyce shouted to Corporal Stone,
standing beside him in an open turret.
'Knew about what?'
'Where we're going, I mean. These Ardennes,'
Boyce said and, remembering other battles,
ran the tip of his tongue over dry lips.

*HQ 33 Armoured Brigade, Belgium, 1944*
*Jim Hovell*


# In the Land where Tanks

In the land
Where tanks had plowed the soil,
A little flower stands in a can
On the altar in front of the Madonna
Inside a ruined chapel.

The little flower
With head bowed down
Sticks up out of the can,
Out of an emptied can
That once held baby food.

And through the damaged roof
The clouded sky, like a good neighbour,
Benevolently pours
Rainwater into the can.
And in a mirror of water
The Holy Virgin contemplates herself.
Half hidden in a niche,
Resembling a foreigner herself,
In the land
Where tanks had plowed the soil.

*Leonid Martynov*
*translated from the Russian by George Reavey*


# Terra Australis

Here, and here only in an age of iron,
The dreamers are proved right;
No armies underlie these rolling fields,
No lost loves haunt the night,
Nor can the farmer, turning with his spade,
Bring shard or helm to light.

Innocence, clad in born and faded gold,
Walks up and down these hills
Where unobtrusive flickering flowers rebuke
The show of daffodils:
With sombre colours and with sparse designs
Acre on acre fills.

Paradise lingers like a tapestry:
The web has not been torn;
Luther and Cromwell, Socrates and Marx
Have never yet been born,
Nor did a glowing Florence rise to shape
The European dawn.

We are the final children of the earth
Whom knowledge has not scarred,
Delighting still in sunlight and green grass
Back in our own backyard:
Gaping, we hear the tales of adulthood
Where life is dour and hard,

Far, far away, beyond some wicked wood.

*Chris Wallace-Crabbe*


# Memory

When I was young my heart and head were light,
And I was gay and feckless as a colt
Out in the fields, with morning in the may,
Wind on the grass, wings in the orchard bloom.
   O thrilling sweet, my joy, when life was free
   And all the paths led on from hawthorn-time
   Across the carolling meadows into June.

But now my heart is heavy-laden. I sit
Burning my dreams away beside the fire:
For death has made me wise and bitter and strong;
And I am rich in all that I have lost.
   O starshine on the fields of long-ago,
   Bring me the darkness and the nightingale;
   Dim wealds of vanished summer, peace of home,
   And silence; and the faces of my friends.

*Siegfried Sassoon*

# Departure

We take it with us, the cry
of a train slicing a field
leaving its stiff suture, a distant
tenderness as when rails slip
behind us and our windows
touch the field, where it seems
the dead are awake and so reach
for each other. Your hand
cups the light of a match
to your mouth, to mine, and I want
to ask if the dead hold
their mouths in their hands like this
to know what is left of them.
Between us, a tissue of smoke,
a bundle of belongings, luggage
that will seem to float beside us,
the currency we will change
and change again. Here is the name
of a friend who will take you in,
the papers of a man who vanished,
the one you will become when
the man you have been disappears.
I am the woman whose photograph
you will not recognize, whose face
emptied your eyes, whose eyes
were brief, like the smallest
of cities we slipped through.

*Carolyn Forché*

# After a War

The outcome? Conflicting rumours
As to what faction murdered
The one who, had he survived,
Might have ruled us without corruption.
Not that it matters now:
We're busy collecting the dead,
Counting them, hard though it is
To be sure what side they were on.
What's left of their bodies and faces
Tells of no need but for burial,
And mutilation was practised
By Right, Left and Centre alike.
As for the children and women
Who knows what they wanted
Apart from the usual things?
Food is scarce now, and men are scarce,
Whole villages burnt to the ground,
New cities in disrepair.

The war is over. Somebody must have won.
Somebody will have won, when peace is declared.

*Michael Hamburger*

# Questions of our Time

When we dream of what has gone before
And what is to come after;
When the sun comes up over the hills in the mornings
And sets the way it rose with the moon and stars;
When at last we hang our weapons upon our mud walls
And weep with joy because the battle is over and won;
When the women who fought with us
Bring water in cracked calabashes
And beckon us to the spot where the water
Should drop, drop by drop, in tearful libation,
Do we know indeed what has gone before
And what is to come after?

When fighting warriors stop to dream
Of what has gone before
And what is to come after,
Does the colour of the sky blunt the sharpness of the sword
Or the rain clouds break the flight of the arrow?

When the little straw-hatted boy
Walks in his own shadow
In the common market-place
And pauses to watch the crook in the young men's backs,
The burden of their insane glories,
He will mutter, 'Perhaps, only perhaps' to our questions—
For truly he has seen nothing of life,
And till too late his bright eyes will see nothing of life
But the weight of wisdom and the wooliness of men—
When he sees the wrinkles around our eyes
And wonders why these tribal marks of the world
Should deface and confuse our real and ancient selves
So early in the day,

He will again mutter 'Perhaps, only perhaps',
And will not understand
Until through the haze he sees us, the fighting tribes,
Clutching our tireless bows
And scanning the vast horizons
With our eager and weather-beaten eyes.

*Kwesi Brew*

But in the last days it shall come to pass,
that the mountain of the house of the Lord
shall be established in the top of the mountains,
and it shall be exalted above the hills;
and people shall flow unto it.
And many nations shall come, and say,
Come, and let us go up to the mountain of the Lord,
and to the house of the God of Jacob;
and he will teach us of his ways,
and we will walk in his paths:
for the law shall go forth of Zion,
and the word of the Lord from Jerusalem.
And he shall judge among many people,
and rebuke strong nations afar off;
and they shall beat their swords into plowshares,
and their spears into pruninghooks:
nation shall not lift up a sword against nation,
neither shall they learn war any more.
But they shall sit every man under his vine
and under his fig tree;
and none shall make them afraid:
for the mouth of the Lord of Hosts hath spoken it.

*Micah 4 : 1–4*
*The Bible: King James Version*


# Peace

Night is o'er England, and the winds are still;
Jasmine and honeysuckle steep the air;
Softly the stars that are all Europe's fill
Her heaven-wide dark with radiancy fair;
That shadowed moon now waxing in the west
Stirs not a rumour in her tranquil seas;
Mysterious sleep has lulled her heart to rest,
Deep even as theirs beneath her churchyard trees.

Secure, serene; dumb now the night-hawk's threat;
The guns' low thunder drumming o'er the tide;
The anguish pulsing in her stricken side. . . .
All is at peace. . . . But, never, heart, forget:
For this her youngest, best, and bravest died,
These bright dews once were mixed with bloody sweat.

*Walter de la Mare*


# I Think Continually

I think continually of those who were truly great.
Who, from the womb, remembered the soul's history
Through corridors of light where the hours are suns
Endless and singing. Whose lovely ambition
Was that their lips, still touched with fire,
Should tell of the Spirit clothed from head to foot in song.
And who hoarded from the Spring branches
The desires falling across their bodies like blossoms.

What is precious, is never to forget
The essential delight of the blood drawn from ageless springs
Breaking through rocks in worlds before our earth.
Never to deny its pleasure in the morning simple light
Nor its grave evening demand for love.
Never to allow gradually the traffic to smother
With noise and fog the flowering of the Spirit.

Near the snow, near the sun, in the highest fields
See how these names are fêted by the waving grass
And by the streamers of white cloud
And whispers of wind in the listening sky.
The names of those who in their lives fought for life,
Who wore at their hearts the fire's centre.
Born of the sun they travelled a short while toward the sun
And left the vivid air signed with their honour.

*Stephen Spender*

# The End

After the blast of lightning from the east,
The flourish of loud clouds, the Chariot Throne;
After the drums of time have rolled and ceased,
And by the bronze west long retreat is blown,

Shall Life renew these bodies? Of a truth
All death will he annul, all tears assuage?—
Or fill these void veins full again with youth,
And wash, with an immortal water, Age?

When I do ask white Age he saith not so:
'My head hangs weighed with snow.'
And when I hearken to the Earth, she saith:
'My fiery heart shinks, aching. It is death.
Mine ancient scars shall not be glorified,
Nor my titanic tears, the seas, be dried.'

*Wilfred Owen*

The people that walked in darkness
have seen a great light:
they that dwell in the land of the shadow of death,
upon them hath the light shined.
Thou hast multiplied the nation,
and not increased the joy:
they joy before thee according to the joy in harvest,
and as men rejoice when they divide the spoil.
For thou hast broken the yoke of his burden,
and the staff of his shoulder,

the rod of his oppressor, as in the day of Midian.
For every battle of the warrior is with confused noise,
and garments rolled in blood;
but this shall be with burning and fuel of fire.
For unto us a child is born,
unto us a son is given:
and the government shall be upon his shoulder:
and his name shall be called Wonderful,
Counsellor, The mighty God,
The everlasting Father, the Prince of Peace.
Of the increase of his government and peace
there shall be no end,
upon the throne of David, and upon his kingdom,
to order it, and to establish it with judgment
and with justice from henceforth even for ever.

*Isaiah 9: 2–7*
*The Bible: King James version*


They held up a stone.
   I said, 'Stone.'
Smiling they said, 'Stone.'

They showed me a tree.
   I said, 'Tree.'
Smiling they said, 'Tree.'

They shed a man's blood.
   I said, 'Blood.'
Smiling they said, 'Paint.'

They shed a man's blood.
   I said, 'Blood.'
Smiling they said, 'Paint.'

*Dannie Abse, adapted from the Hebrew*
*of Amir Gilboa, 1982*

# Nursery Rhyme 1984

'Shall we be there in time?'
  said the child to the stranger.
'You promised I'd see it.'
'You'll see it,' he said.

'Hold my hand tight,'
  said the child, smiling.
'Please don't let me go.'
'I've got you,' he said.

'I'm frightened of fire.
  Are you sure it is safe?'
'Perfectly safe.
  Don't fidget,' he said.

'Will mummy be there
  and daddy and granny?'
'Everyone's going.
  The whole world,' he said.

'Will we dance and sing
  Ring a roses around it?'
'Ring a roses and all
  fall down,' he said.

'It has grown very dark,'
  said her voice to his shadow.
'Are you sure of the way?'
'Quite sure,' he said.

'I'm frightened. I want
  to go home,' said the child.
'I'm not turning back.
  You keep going,' he said.

And I watched them go,
  hand in hand into darkness.
'Any time now.
  Trust me,' he said.

*Paul Coltman*

# Reprisal

They worked all night with cardboard and with wood
to make those dummy planes to hoodwink the foe,
and in the chilly morning solitude
wheeled out the dummies to places they should go
on the dispersal fields, and went away;
the hours passed uneventfully, and even
no reconnaissance planes were overhead that day.
They evacuated in the twilight, just after seven,
and when they'd gone the Germans flew above the drome
and by each plane they dropped a wooden bomb.

*Herbert Corby*


# Lines from 'Locksley Hall'

For I dipt into the future, far as human eye could see,
Saw the Vision of the world, and all the wonder that would
    be;
Saw the heavens fill with commerce, argosies of magic
    sails,
Pilots of the purple twilight, dropping down with costly
    bales;
Heard the heavens fill with shouting, and there rain'd a
    ghastly dew
From the nations' airy navies grappling in the central blue;
Far along the world-wide whisper of the south-wind
    rushing warm,
With the standards of the peoples plunging thro' the
    thunder storm;
Till the war-drum throbb'd no longer, and the battle flags
    were furl'd
In the Parliament of man, the Federation of the world.
There the common sense of most shall hold a fretful realm
    in awe,
And the kindly earth shall slumber, lapt in universal law.

*Alfred, Lord Tennyson*

# The Seed

I am the small million.
I am the locked fountain.

Late, late, in summer's dotage
When they stand gaunt and blasted,
The hollyhock tower and the cottage
Of clover, and age has wasted
The sun—then, then at last
I jump, I glide, a waif
Victoriously lost,
Tempestuously safe.

I go as weak as sea-water.
I lie as quiet as radium.

In the dust-high caravan, in
The cabin of a bird's claw,
Or sheepback I travel, I have been
In the whale, his prophesying maw;
I have occupied both town
And parish, an airborne spirit, a
Soldier in thistledown,
A meek inheritor.

I am dry but I shall slake you
I am hard but I shall satisfy you.

The apple contains me and I
Contain the apple, I balance
A field on a stalk and tie
A century's voices in silence;
And all the hopes of the happy
And all the sighs of the sorry
Rest in my power to copy
And copying vary.

I am the first omega.
I am the last alpha.

And remember, I lie beneath
All soils of time, fears' frost;
Remember, I stir in my death,
Most missed I am least lost;
Remember, in the gaunt garden
In the kingdom of a broken tree
You will find after Armageddon,
After the deluge, me.

*Hal Summers*


# As I walked out one Evening

As I walked out one evening,
    Walking down Bristol Street,
The crowds upon the pavement
    Were fields of harvest wheat.

And down by the brimming river
    I heard a lover sing
Under an arch of the railway:
    'Love has no ending.

'I'll love you, dear, I'll love you
    Till China and Africa meet,
And the river jumps over the mountain
    And the salmon sing in the street,

'I'll love you till the ocean
    Is folded and hung up to dry
And the seven stars go squawking
    Like geese about the sky.

The years shall run like rabbits,
    For in my arms I hold
The Flower of the Ages,
    And the first love of the world.'

But all the clocks in the city
    Began to whirr and chime:
'O let not Time deceive you,
    You cannot conquer Time.

'In the burrows of the Nightmare
    Where Justice naked is,
Time watches from the shadow
    And coughs when you would kiss.

'In headaches and in worry
    Vaguely life leaks away,
And Time will have his fancy
    To-morrow or to-day.

'Into many a green valley
    Drifts the appalling snow;
Time breaks the threaded dances
    And the diver's brilliant bow.

'O plunge your hands in water,
    Plunge them in up to the wrist;
Stare, stare in the basin
    And wonder what you've missed.

'The glacier knocks in the cupboard,
    The desert sighs in the bed,
And the crack in the teacup opens
    A lane to the land of the dead.

'Where the beggars raffle the banknotes
    And the Giant is enchanting to Jack,
And the Lily-white Boy is a Roarer,
    And Jill goes down on her back.

'O look, look in the mirror,
    O look in your distress;
Life remains a blessing
    Although you cannot bless.

'O stand, stand at the window
 As the tears scald and start;
You shall love your crooked neighbour
 With your crooked heart.'

It was late, late in the evening,
 The lovers they were gone;
The clocks had ceased their chiming,
 And the deep river ran on.

*W. H. Auden*


# In Time of 'The Breaking of Nations'

### I
Only a man harrowing clods
 In a slow silent walk
With an old horse that stumbles and nods
 Half asleep as they stalk.

### II
Only thin smoke without flame
 From the heaps of couch-grass;
Yet this will go onward the same
 Though Dynasties pass.

### III
Yonder a maid and her wight
 Come whispering by:
War's annals will cloud into night
 Ere their story die.

*Thomas Hardy*

# How Sweet the Night

How sweet, how sweet will be the night
When windows that are black and cold
Kindle anew with fires of gold;

When dusk in quiet shall descend
And darkness come once more a friend;

When wings pursue their proper flight
And bring not terror but delight;

When clouds are innocent again
And hide no storms of deadly rain;

When the round sky is swept of wars
And keeps but gentle moon and stars.

Lord, who doth even now prepare
That peaceful sky, that harmless air—
How sweet, how sweet shall be the night!

*Rachael Bates*

# 'There Will Come Soft Rains'

There will come soft rains and the smell of the ground,
And swallows calling with their shimmering sound;

And frogs in the pools singing at night,
And wild-plum trees in tremulous white;

Robins will wear their feathery fire
Whistling their whims on a low fence-wire;

And not one will know of the war, not one
Will care at last when it is done.

Not one would mind, neither bird nor tree,
If mankind perished utterly;

And Spring herself, when she woke at dawn,
Would scarcely know that we were gone.

*Sara Teasdale*

# Index of titles and first lines

# Acknowledgements

The editors and publisher are grateful for permission to include the following material.

**Dannie Abse**: 'They held up a stone' from *Way Out In the Centre* (Hutchinson). Reprinted by permission of Anthony Sheil Associates Ltd. **Aeschylus**: from *The Persians* translated by G. M. Cookson (Everyman's Library). Reprinted by permission of J. M. Dent & Sons Ltd. **Bella Akhmadulina**: 'Small Aircraft' from *A Book of Women Poets From Antiquity to Now* (Schocken Books, 1980). **Mabel Esther Allan**: 'I saw a Broken Town' from *The Haunted Valley* and Other Poems, copyright Mabel Esther Allan 1981 (privately printed). Also in *Chaos of the Night* (Virago, 1984). Reprinted by permission of the author. First published, *Poetry Quarterly*, 1941. **Mary Desirée Anderson**: 'The Black-Out' from *Bow Bells Are Silent* (Williams & Norgate Ltd.). **Herbert Asquith**: 'The Volunteer' from *Poems 1912–33(1934)*. Reprinted by permission of Sidgwick & Jackson Ltd. **W. H. Auden**: 'On this Island', copyright 1937 and renewed 1965 by W. H. Auden; 'Some Say that Love's a Little Boy', copyright 1940 and renewed 1968 by W. H. Auden: 'Epitaph on a Tyrant', copyright 1940 and renewed 1968 by W. H. Auden; and 'As I Walked out one Evening', copyright 1940 and renewed 1960 by W. H. Auden, from *Collected Poems*, edited by Edward Mendelson. Reprinted by permission of Faber & Faber Ltd., and Random House Inc. **Donald Bain**: 'War Poet' from *Poems of the Second World War* (Dent/ Salamander Oasis Trust), edited by Victor Selwyn. Used with permission. **Rachel Bates**: 'How Sweet the Night' from *Songs From a Lake* (Hutchinson). Reprinted by permission of the Century Hutchinson Publishing Group Ltd. **Patricia Beer**: 'Waterloo' from *The Lie of the Land*; 'Return to Sedgemoor' from *Selected Poems*. Both reprinted by permission of Century Hutchinson Ltd. **Martin Bell**: 'Reason for Refusal' from *Complete Poems* by Martin Bell, edited by Peter Porter (Bloodaxe Books Ltd., 1988). Reprinted by permission of the publisher. **John Betjeman**: '1940' from *Uncollected Poems*. Reprinted by permission of John Murray (Publishers) Ltd. **Alexander Blok**: 'The Kite' from *Poems from the Russian*, translated by Frances Cornford and Esther Polianowsky. Reprinted by permission of Faber & Faber Ltd. **Kwesi Brew**: 'Questions of Our Time' from *Commonwealth Poets of Today* (The English Association). **Charles Causley**: 'At the British War Cemetery, Bayeux' from *Union Street* (Rupert Hart-Davis, 1957). Reprinted by permission of David Higham Associates Ltd. **C. P. Cavafy**: 'Waiting for the Barbarians' from *Collected Poems* by C. P. Cavafy translated by Edmund Keeley and Philip Sherrard, ed. George Savidis. Translation copyright © 1975 by Edmund Keeley and Philip Sherrard. Reprinted by permission of the Hogarth Press and Princeton University Press. **Lois Clark**: 'Picture from the Blitz' from *Another Dimension* (Outposts Publications). **Gillian Clarke**: 'Lunchtime Lecture' from *Selected Poems*. Reprinted by permission of Carcanet Press Ltd. **Paul Coltman**: 'Troy', 'Hieronymous Bosch, we can do it', 'Cissbury Ring' and 'Nursery Rhyme 1984' from *A Momentary Stay* (Peterloo Poets, 1985). Reprinted by permission. **Robert Conquest**: 'Poem in 1944' from *New and Collected Poems* (Century Hutchinson, 1988). Reprinted by permission of the author. **Herbert Corby**: 'Reprisal' from *Hampdens Going Over* (Fortune Press/Charles Skilton Ltd.). Reprinted with permission. **E. E. Cummings**: 'i thank You God . . .' from *Complete Poems 1913–1962*, copyright 1947 by E. E. Cummings; renewed 1975 by Nancy T. Andrews. Reprinted by permission of Grafton Books – A Division of the Collins Publishing Group, and Harcourt Brace Jovanovich, Inc. 'next to of course god america i' from *Complete Poems 1913–1962*, published in the US in *Is: 5 poems by E. E. Cummings* edited.by George James Firmage, copyright 1926 by Horace Liveright, copyright 1954 by E. E. Cummings, copyright © 1985 by E. E. Cummings Trust, © 1985 by George James Firmage. Reprinted by permission of Grafton Books and Liveright Publishing, Corporation. **Paul Dehn**: 'Armistice' from *The Fern on the Rock*. Reprinted by permission of James Bernard. **Walter de la Mare**: 'Peace' from *The Complete Poems of Walter de la Mare*. Reprinted by permission of The Literary Trustees of Walter de la Mare and The Society of Authors as their representative. **Emily Dickinson**: 'It feels a shame to be Alive-. . .' Reprinted by permission of the publishers and the Trustees of Amherst College from *The Poems of Emily Dickinson*, edited by Thomas H. Johnson, Cambridge, Mass.: The Belknap Press of Harvard University Press, copyright 1951, © 1955, 1979, 1983 by The President and Fellows of Harvard College, and from *The Complete Poems of Emily Dickinson*, edited by Thomas H. Johnson, copyright 1929 by Martha Dickinson Bianchi, copyright © renewed 1957 by Mary L. Hampson, by permission of Little, Brown and Company. **Keith**